In the Shadow of Karl Barth: Charlotte von Kirschbaum

In the Shadow of Karl Barth: Charlotte von Kirschbaum

Renate Köbler

Translated by
Keith Crim

WIPF & STOCK · Eugene, Oregon

Wipf and Stock Publishers
199 W 8th Ave, Suite 3
Eugene, OR 97401

In the Shadow of Karl Barth
Charlotte von Kirschbaum
By Kobler, Renata and Crim, Keith
Copyright©1987 by Kobler, Renata
ISBN 13: 978-1-62564-342-1
Publication date 8/31/2013
Previously published by WJK, 1987

Contents

Illustrations	7
Translator's Preface	9
Preface	11
Prologue by Rose Marie Barth	15
Introduction	21
1. Childhood and Youth	23
2. Georg Merz, "a Good Friend in the Early Years"	25
3. Bergli, a Place of Encounter	28
4. Stations on the Way to Shared Theological Work	31
5. Bergli, a Place of Shared Work	35
6. Time Together, Work Together	38
7. A Suitable Counterpart and Helper	41

8.	Confessing the Faith in the Church's Struggle	46
9.	Committed Service in Swiss Exile	50
10.	Toward a Free and Independent Germany	54
11.	An Immeasurable Contribution	58
12.	Charlotte von Kirschbaum—*"Die wirkliche Frau"?*	63
13.	As Her Strength Failed	70
14.	"A Long, Slow Departure"	74

Lectures by Charlotte von Kirschbaum 79

    "Address for the Movement 'Free Germany,'" 1945   81

    "The Role of Women in the Proclamation of the Word," 1951   93

Epilogue by Hans Prolingheuer   125

Notes   141

Bibliography   151

Index of Names   155

Illustrations

1. At Karl Barth's side — 20
2. Karl Barth in a quiet moment — 26
3. With Eduard Thurneysen — 29
4. Charlotte in 1926 — 32
5. Charlotte and Gertrude Staewen — 34
6. With Karl Barth in the study at Bergli — 37
7. Working together — 39
8. Charlotte in 1929 — 43
9. Traveling together — 44
10. Charlotte in Basel, 1943, age 44 — 52
11. With council members Langhoff and Abegg — 56
12. Outside the house in the Pilgerstrasse, 1948 — 61
13. At Le Croisie, April 1950 — 68
14. Sonnenhalde Sanatorium — 72
15. The Barth family grave — 76
16. Caricature of church leaders opposing Barth — 126

Translator's Preface

After receiving the B.D. and Th.M. at Union Theological Seminary in Virginia I spent the academic year 1951–52 at the University of Basel in advanced study in Old Testament. That major interest, however, could not keep me away from Karl Barth's lectures in theology and his English language seminar. There, at his home in the Pilgerstrasse, I first met Charlotte von Kirschbaum. Like many other foreign students, I wondered about her relationship with Karl Barth. There was gossip at the time; how much, I did not know until I read Renate Köbler's book. One thing was clear: this attractive and brilliant woman occupied a major place in Barth's life and work.

I had only a few opportunities to talk with her, and no opportunity to get to know her personally. Three and half decades later, when Renate Köbler's book first came into my hands, I read it eagerly and urged Westminster/John Knox Press to publish it. It gives me a great deal of pleasure now to present it to a wider circle of readers, in partial payment of the debt we all owe to Karl Barth and Charlotte von Kirschbaum.

KEITH CRIM

For some are in the darkness

And some are in the light,

And we see the ones in light;

Those in the dark we do not see.

—Bertold Brecht,
to the melody of "Mack the Knife"

Preface

Charlotte von Kirschbaum, in the shadow of Karl Barth: this title may cause some amazement. A theologian of our century who did not seek recognition through publication for herself, she nevertheless, in her life and work, exerted a major influence on one of the greatest theological works of the twentieth century, that of Karl Barth.

Charlotte von Kirschbaum is a woman who thus far has found little recognition from researchers into the history of the church and of theology, a woman whose life has been, at most, mere grist for the theological gossip mills.

Hans Prolingheuer first called my attention to the name of Charlotte von Kirschbaum, which until then had been completely unknown to me. In the summer semester of 1984, thanks to the initiative of some deeply committed students, he was invited to lecture at the University of Marburg. He gave to us who were studying there the privilege of being the first group to discuss his book *Kleine politische Kirchengeschichte* ("A Brief Political History of the Church"), which had just been published. During that semester we were concerned with the as yet little-studied political side of the Protestant churches' struggle against the Nazi regime, and I had had to correct my previously naïve picture of the

Confessing Church, learning slowly and also painfully to distinguish among its various faces.

When I told Mr. Prolingheuer that I wanted to write my seminar paper on the activities of women in recent Protestant church history, a field where little research had been done, and asked his advice, he mentioned Charlotte von Kirschbaum's name. The limited information about her in the Barth biography by Eberhard Busch further aroused my curiosity.

Since there had been no publication dealing with her, and since if she is mentioned at all in the literature it is only marginally, I needed to make contact first of all with those who had known her personally. I was able to talk with Karl Barth's oldest son, Professor Markus Barth, and his wife, Mrs. Rose Marie Barth, who was a close friend and confidant of Charlotte von Kirschbaum; with Professor Eberhard Busch, former student and research assistant to Barth and author of the extensive Barth biography; with Wolf von Kirschbaum, nephew of Charlotte; and with her close friends Professor Helmut Gollwitzer and Dr. Lili Simon, who came to know her while they were students in Basel.

All of them were able to bring this woman to life for me through their accounts. As I endeavored to think myself into her situation and to understand and feel what her world was like, her thoughts, the way of life she chose for herself, it became my ambition to present the testimony of as many of her contemporaries as possible. My research paper became a biography of Charlotte von Kirschbaum, her life and her work, written from my perspective as a woman concerned to present a critically informed view: a work of a sympathetic partisan, according to the principles of contemporary feminist research.

I sent the finished manuscript to all those whose help I had sought, with the request that they read it critically and make suggestions for supplementing or correcting it. Mr. Prolingheuer encouraged me to rework the material with a view to its eventual publication, and it is through his efforts that this book appears now.

In the process of revision I considered all the suggestions made by those from whom I had received information. In addition, an article of mine in the journal *Junge Kirche* drew many written responses from persons who had known Charlotte von Kirschbaum and Karl Barth personally. As far as was possible, I made the suggested changes.

In addition to the published works listed in the bibliography I have listed separately, as sources, my conversations in person or by telephone with those persons and my letters from them, as well as some unpublished documents.

It has been my concern to liberate Charlotte von Kirschbaum, as a theological partner and "suitable companion" to Karl Barth, from the shadow existence that became her lot after her death. [For this reason, the second half of the book includes two of her articles, an "Address for the Movement 'Free Germany' " and "The Role of Women in the Proclamation of the Word"—TR.] My hope in addition is that I can make a small contribution to a neglected part of Barth's biography and of Barth research.

I would like to thank all those who share my concern and who through personal conversations or written communication were of great help to me in sketching the life of this woman. My special thanks go to Wolf von Kirschbaum, who helped in the launching of my book and who graciously provided me with photographs of his aunt.

I must also not fail to thank those who made contributions from the shadows: Hans Prolingheuer, for making my work possible and supporting it throughout; my friends Peter Winzen and Esther Rohr, who accompanied me on some of my travels and were valued partners in conversation; and, not least, my friend Petra Rodenhausen, who was of great help in the preparation of my manuscript.

Material in brackets within a quotation has been added by the author. Where there is more than one quotation in a sentence, the note that follows applies to them all.

Prologue

It was the winter semester of 1937–38. Barely three years had passed since Karl Barth had been removed from his teaching position in Bonn and returned to his hometown of Basel as professor in the university there. The Church College in Berlin was closed, and Martin Niemöller had already been in a concentration camp for three months. Karl Barth was giving his lectures on the exegesis of 1 Peter. Many German students, some of them in their advanced semesters, others in their early semesters but older in years (these were mostly Jewish students in jurisprudence), and a sprinkling of worthy Swiss filled the classroomlike hall on the Upper Stapfelberg, not far from the old university on the Rhine. Eagerly I took my place behind a small pleasant-looking woman, a good ten years older than I was, hardly a student but an intent listener. When I spoke to her a few weeks later, I invited her to visit me and asked for advice about what to do after finishing my training as a nurse. Would it be better to attend a school of social work for women in order to become a parish assistant or to plunge directly into the study of theology? She answered, "If you are interested in what is really going on in theology, then you must study theology."

This was Lollo, Charlotte von Kirschbaum, and I followed her advice in a manner different from what she and I had intended. For soon thereafter I found myself in the Barth household as Markus Barth's fiancée and met her again as "Aunt Lollo."

Eduard Thurneysen, then pastor of the cathedral in Basel, who had confirmed me and followed the subsequent course of my life, advised me, even before I became personally acquainted with my future parents-in-law, not to meddle in that which was the responsibility of the older generation. By this he meant the situation in which Mama and Papa Barth lived together under one roof with "Aunt Lollo." He told me that the relationship among these three persons was unique, something that had developed over the years, and I should simply accept it as such without question. I should love each of the three of them for himself or herself. At the time I had only a vague idea of what he was talking about, but I soon learned that he was right and his advice was good. The less that gossips in Basel, and especially elsewhere, knew about the house on the Albanring, the more they found to talk about. None of them had any idea how much suffering there was under the roof of that house. But the work of theology was joyful, and the involvement in that work, to whatever extent, held the three together through toils and perils.

In later years Lollo could still say, "You know, he called me to him"—as if I had ever doubted it! It was obvious that Karl Barth needed her urgently, not merely as a competent secretary who took down each of his lectures from dictation and wrote them out for the printer, who handled most of his correspondence and kept his records and minutes, but who was first and foremost the companion of his busy life. No day passed without important letters from friends or advice seekers, without decisions to be made. Her keen understanding of human nature and her friendliness were of help to many, as were her loving criticism and comforting patience, but most of all to Karl Barth.

Prologue by Rose Marie Barth

In all this she never thought she was treated unfairly or was unable to "realize" herself in any respect. She was realistic enough to know that she could not have her cake and eat it too. And she saw the demands that were placed upon her as noble enough to challenge all her abilities and all her strength. Her greatest and deepest interest, to know what was really going on in theology, was caught up in the progress of Karl Barth's theological thought and research. His work was her work. Her participation, her understanding, her intuition, her contribution, her admonition, her agreement—these became a part of their common labors and, in turn, shaped her. In all this she felt accepted, valued, loved, not only by Karl Barth but by everyone who knew her.

Her life was lived in the shadows. She did not look at it that way; to do so would have seemed to her gross ingratitude. But the truth is that her life was not only lived in the shadows, it ended in night. It was a slow approach of the night, however, in great peace. A physician friend of hers had prophesied at the beginning of the road she traveled with Karl Barth that she could not bear up under a life based on this sort of call. It broke her, but she lived it. And it was not a mournful journey.

Basel, 1986 ROSE MARIE BARTH

In the Shadow of Karl Barth:
Charlotte von Kirschbaum

1. At Karl Barth's side.

Introduction

This woman at Karl Barth's side is Charlotte von Kirschbaum. She stands beside him but in the background, half in shadow. She observes him attentively and follows his work with her eyes. Perhaps she has just placed a document before him for his evaluation. For almost forty years she was Barth's closest associate—standing at his side. But today she stands in the background, in the shadows.

Work in the shadows[1] is work that is done in silence, hidden from view, not included in the histories of our time. Work in the shadows is work that is indispensable because it creates postulates, lays foundations. It is the work done by many at the second level of the scholarly hierarchy. It is work that never receives public notice. Work in the shadows is the work that countless women, especially housewives, perform without pay, work that keeps our economic system functioning. Work in the shadows is work that is not seen, that knows little recognition or appreciation.

Charlotte von Kirschbaum performed work in the shadows. Karl Barth was himself aware of her great significance. In his preface to the *Church Dogmatics* III/3 he wrote:

> I should not like to conclude this Preface without expressly drawing the attention of readers of these

seven volumes to what they and I owe to the twenty years of work quietly accomplished at my side by Charlotte von Kirschbaum. She has devoted no less of her life and powers to the growth of this work than I have myself. Without her co-operation it could not have been advanced from day to day, and I should hardly dare contemplate the future which may yet remain to me. I know what it really means to have a helper.[2]

Charlotte von Kirschbaum was a theologian of our century who never studied theology in a university. With her life and her labor she participated in and helped shape the development of the history of theology in this century. But in spite of this, the woman and her accomplishments remain largely unknown. So far there have been no publications that deal with her. Only in two Barth biographies[3] is she even mentioned as Barth's co-worker, and the extent of her influence is only hinted at. In the biography written by Gerhard Wehr[4] her name is not mentioned at all.

Hardly anyone today knows of her existence. Her name is unfamiliar to the students of my generation. Only a few persons are still living who knew her personally and who hold vivid memories of her.

In writing this book it is my intention to free Charlotte von Kirschbaum from the "obscurity into which some are pharisaically thankful she has fallen"[5] and to keep her memory fresh, so that she will no longer be one of the innumerable forgotten women of history.

1
Childhood and Youth

We know very little about Charlotte von Kirschbaum as a child. In later years she seldom spoke of this time[1], and this in itself says much.
Named Charlotte Emilie Henriette Eugenie, she was born on July 25, 1899, in Ingolstadt, Bavaria, the only daughter of Major General Maximilian von Kirschbaum and his wife, Henriette, Baroness von Bruck.[2] But she by no means enjoyed the well-protected life of a young member of the nobility, as her name might lead us to believe. With her two brothers, Max, born in 1897, and Hans, born in 1902, she was raised in the "stilted atmosphere of an officer's household."[3]
She grew up at a time when educational opportunities for girls were still quite limited and by no means comparable to those available to boys. She felt very close to her father, who early recognized and encouraged her intellectual gifts.[4] Her mother, on the other hand, was often sickly and was quite close to Charlotte's two brothers.[5] The mother was jealous of the special relationship her husband had with Charlotte, and this led to a strained relationship between mother and daughter.[6]
Charlotte experienced the fate typical of children of military personnel—transferred, and transferred again. Soon after her birth her family moved from Ingolstadt to Munich, where they lived in the Mars-

strasse, but they did not remain there long. In following years the family lived, always for only a short time, in Ulm and in Amberg in the Oberpfalz, so that during her childhood Charlotte never could feel that any place was truly home. Quite early she became accustomed to a life of wandering.

Only at the beginning of the First World War did the family finally settle in Munich. There Charlotte completed in 1915 the six-year course of higher education for young women at the Anna Lyceum and received her diploma, which at that time did not qualify the graduate for entry to a university.[7]

During the war she earned her pocket money working for the army office for mail censorship.[8] The sudden death of her father, who was killed in battle in France in 1916[9] while serving as commander of the Sixth Bavarian Infantry Division, was a severe blow and complicated her family situation.[10] The shortage of food during and after the war resulted in serious harm to her health.[11]

"After the end of the war she wanted to become a deaconess, but when she entered her mother's home in Augsburg the unexpected atmosphere came as a shock." That same day she decided to enter training as a nurse with the German Red Cross[12] and left home to begin her training in Munich. Here she formed a close friendship with Emmy Lentrodt, with whom she shared many interests, including a deep interest in theology.

On finishing her training, she served as a Red Cross nurse in a children's clinic in Munich.[13]

2
Georg Merz, "a Good Friend in the Early Years"

As a young nursing student, Charlotte von Kirschbaum became acquainted with Lutheran pastor Georg Merz (1892–1959). She attended services in his church, and he recognized and encouraged her interest in theology.[1] "Merz moved as a many-sided person in the intellectually exciting circles of the Munich of that day"[2] and had gathered around him a circle of intellectuals including, among others, Thomas Mann. In these circles the intellectual, cultural, political, and theological developments of the period were discussed, and Charlotte von Kirschbaum took an active part in these activities.[3] Belonging to this circle meant much to her and influenced—even determined—the future course of her life. Here her intellectual and spiritual capabilities could come alive, and she found an access to theology she could never have known in her mother's home. Georg Merz, who became a companion in her journey (much later she herself called him "a good friend in the early years"),[4] played a key role in her development at this stage. Through him, she first came in contact with Karl Barth's theology.

Merz, who in addition to his work as pastor was a theological consultant for the Christian Kaiser publishing house in Munich, had become aware of Barth's *Letter to the Romans* as early as 1919. This book became for him a "transforming discovery."[5]

He wrote an enthusiastic review, which he promptly sent to Barth in Safenwil.[6] Barth felt that Merz understood him, and they became friends. The two men entered into a regular correspondence, visited each other, and in 1921 Merz stood as godfather for Barth's fourth child, Robert Matthias.[7]

In August 1922, Barth, Eduard Thurneysen, and Friedrich Gogarten decided to start a new theological journal with the name *Zwischen den Zeiten* ("Between the Times"), and Merz was chosen as editor.[8] He supervised the editing of this famous series of articles until the end of 1933, when publication was suspended because of the break between Barth and Gogarten, which also involved Thurneysen as Barth's theological partner.

In addition, the increasingly nationalistic and conservative stance that Merz adopted during the years of the church struggle resulted in tensions between him and Barth. Barth wrote, "Georg Merz, like so many others, had so completely reverted to his ori-

2. Karl Barth in a quiet moment.

gins (in this case, Bavarian-Frankish-Lutheran) that though I was able to maintain relations with him as a person, I could no longer be in unity with him on the issues we faced."[9] This human bond, the friendship between them, remained intact till their final meeting in June 1957.[10] That final visit with their sick friend Georg Merz greatly distressed Charlotte von Kirschbaum because he was suffering from severe sclerosis.[11]

It was to be expected that Merz, as an enthusiastic supporter of Barth, would discuss in his Munich circle the new current of Swiss thought, which, beginning with Barth's lecture in Tambach, was now attracting attention in Germany. We can be certain that Barth's *Letter to the Romans* was handed around and thus fell into the hands of Charlotte von Kirschbaum. Because of her curiosity about theology she continued to follow Karl Barth, and we may assume that she read with great interest each new issue of *Zwischen den Zeiten*.

When she finally met Barth for the first time, Charlotte had long since been acquainted with the beginnings of dialectic theology and in addition had probably learned from Merz something about Barth as a person. A first brief encounter probably took place at a lecture of Barth's that she attended in the company of Georg Merz. It is also probable that in a conversation after the lecture Barth invited her to a meeting with Merz in Switzerland.[12] Charlotte gladly accepted the invitation, and in the summer of 1924 she took a vacation at Bergli to rest from her strenuous work load.[13] Surely she did not yet dream that at Bergli a whole new phase of her life would begin.

3
Bergli, a Place of Encounter

On July 21, 1925,[1] Charlotte von Kirschbaum traveled again to Switzerland in the company of Georg Merz and visited Lake Zurich. The first purpose of this journey was to restore her health,[2] which had been strained by the demands of her work.

On a height called Bergli ("little mountain") overlooking Lake Zurich, Barth's friends Ruedi and Gerty Pestalozzi had built a modest summer home. Here Merz and Charlotte received a friendly welcome. Ever since it was built, this place had been a favorite spot for Barth, as it had also been for Thurneysen; each year Barth made it his summer home. In addition, Barth's friends and acquaintances were always made welcome there by the hospitable Pestalozzis. It was not only a place for rest and friendly gatherings but also a place where much hard work was performed. It was Barth's custom to prepare or revise his class lectures, essays, and public lectures there.[3]

Karl Barth had been professor for Reformed Theology in Göttingen, but at the end of the spring semester, 1925, he was called to the University of Münster. Charlotte von Kirschbaum now came to know him better and was accepted into his inner circle. At Bergli, too, began her enduring friendship with the Pestalozzis, especially with Gerty, a many-sided, highly cultured woman. From 1924 on, Char-

Bergli, a Place of Encounter

lotte spent her summers at Bergli.[4] Each year she grew closer to this circle of friends, especially to Karl Barth and his thought.

In the summer of 1925, Eduard Thurneysen also spent some time at Bergli. Shortly after his return home he wrote a letter to Barth in which he said:

On Friday we spent yet another fine day at Bergli with the Merzes and Miss von Kirschbaum, who remained there until Sunday morning. Georg is truly irreplaceable as the manager of our group. If only he spent more time with the work; but he does have a full load of things to do. Really, Lempp [Albert Lempp, head of the Christian Kaiser publishing house] *should engage Miss von Kirschbaum as a secretary for Merz. She could take over much of the correspondence, contacts with authors, and the like, and certainly that would be as good a place for her as nursing.*[5]

3. With Eduard Thurneysen.

This did not come to pass, but still in that summer the idea was born that they should make it possible for Charlotte to receive further education. She herself had surely reached the decision to do so before this visit to Bergli.[6] Rudolf Pestalozzi was owner of an ironworks in Zurich and supported Barth in many things. Here too he responded by providing financial support for this project.[7]

4
Stations on the Way to Shared Theological Work

Before the end of 1925, Charlotte von Kirschbaum had probably already entered the Business School for Women in Munich,[1] where she was trained for secretarial work, a program she "completed with high commendation."[2] After this study she gave up her work as a nurse and took a position as a social worker in the Siemens Works in Nürnberg. There she became acquainted with the "wide-ranging problems of the world of industrial work,"[3] an experience that clearly influenced her political views.

She continued to be in regular correspondence with Karl Barth, who had been teaching in Münster since October 25, 1925. His wife, Nelly, and his five children could not follow him immediately, because the sale of their house dragged on. Charlotte visited him in Münster in February 1926.[4] This visit seems to have been a key date in the development of the relationship between them. They spoke openly of what they felt for one another and determined—while acknowledging the obligations of Barth's marriage—to remain in contact.[5]

In the meantime Barth had begun to revise the lectures in theology that he had given in Göttingen and to give them "new form." He sent his manuscripts first of all to Charlotte.[6] After giving them a critical reading she sent them to Thurneysen, who had already been Barth's helper and counsel in the

4. Charlotte in 1926.

preparation of the *Epistle to the Romans*. It was now his responsibility to check through this new work and decide whether it was ready for publication.[7] At Barth's instructions, Charlotte also sent the manuscript to Georg Merz, who "for the sake of his feelings of prestige" should also have a say in "whether the thing should be published."[8]

For this project of Barth's, Charlotte not only undertook the secretarial work but also served as an intermediary and transmitter of messages among Barth, Thurneysen, and Merz.[9] Moreover, her advice was not considered unimportant. Although Merz was against it, she supported Thurneysen in recommending that the material be published.[10]

In August 1927 she traveled with the Barth family to Noschenrode in the Harz Mountains, where the family spent their summer holiday. During this vacation time she helped Barth prepare "his first specifically dogmatic work" for the printer. It was

Stations on the Way to Shared Theological Work 33

designed as the "first volume of a series originally planned to run to several volumes of 'Christian Dogmatics.' "[11] In a letter to Thurneysen, Barth said of this "holiday" that "in addition at least Lollo and I have our hands full with the Dogmatics so that our days are caught up in the same steady tempo—interrupted by pleasant strolls in twos or threes, by visits in the evening to inns, etc., much like the times you have shared with us."[12] After this strenuous work they permitted themselves a short trip of two days on the Rhine before Charlotte returned home.[13]

During the preceding years she had prepared herself more and more for theological study through her association with Karl Barth, so now, for a second time, this time in Berlin, she attended a preparatory school in order to acquire the diploma needed for admission to a university. At this school it was possible to take a so-called examination for the gifted, which required the writing of a thesis. Barth quietly served as her ghostwriter.[14]

During this time Charlotte made the acquaintance of Gertrud Staewen,[15] a social worker in Berlin who had first met Karl Barth in 1922. In a conversation with Brigitte Gollwitzer and Friedrich Marquardt, Gertrud Staewen told them that, after her encounter with Barth, "I discovered the *Letter to the Romans*. I read in it night after night, shouting as I read. . . . That was the real turning point in my life."[16] Under the Nazi regime she worked as a parish assistant in the congregation of the Confessing Church in Berlin-Dahlem. She took an active part in the resistance by forming with her friends Helene Jacobs and Melanie Steinmetz an illegal organization for aiding Jews. After the war she dedicated her efforts to her work in the Tegel prison in Berlin as "Mother of the Ganoven." In 1984 she celebrated her ninetieth birthday.[17]

Gertrud had been a member of Barth's circle before Charlotte was, and the two soon became good

5. Charlotte and Gertrude Staewen.

friends. In a sketch of her remembrances of Charlotte she said of her, "I can see her before me, living in my memory just as she was in those years when I first knew her—it must have been around 1929. In full bright-blue silk dresses which matched so well her marvelous blue eyes, delicate, with fine features, and sparkling with an energy that was never loud but was always present: that energy, that courage for living, with which she had decided once and for all to be there for only one person, for his work, for his well-being and his happiness, for his friends and students."[18]

5
Bergli, a Place of Shared Work

In the spring of 1929 the University of Münster granted Karl Barth a leave of one semester. He used this time, from the middle of April to the end of September, to withdraw to Bergli, where he worked intensively. During this summer Charlotte von Kirschbaum helped him expand his file of quotations.[1] She read theological works and made excerpts from them, an activity that continued to be part of her responsibility. This responsibility went far beyond the work of a secretary. It demanded independent thinking, the ability to discover interconnections and to draw theological conclusions from them. It is certain that without Charlotte von Kirschbaum's work Barth's files "would not have become the instrument that they indeed were."[2]

During these months Charlotte busied herself especially with Luther's sermons. In a letter of May 30, 1928, Barth wrote to Thurneysen, "I must tell you that Lollo has developed uncanny diligence in her work on Luther, and every day she brings to light a great mass of important notes about the sayings of this man that are hidden away in the volumes of his sermons and stores them in my barn."[3] In addition she worked with Kierkegaard's philosophy and made excerpts from the book on Kierkegaard written by the Jesuit Erich Przywara, for whom Barth felt great respect.[4] At the same time the two of them helped each other learn Latin and English.[5]

The distinctive way in which they worked together was described by Gertrud Staewen, who, with the exception of the war years, spent her holidays at Bergli. Before and after their daily walks at Bergli, for which Charlotte always assumed the responsibility,

> they were seen in the "Törli" ["little tower"], the two rooms which Ruedi had built for them so that they could work undisturbed. There they sat at the desk by the large window, Lollo at the typewriter as she handed him a few pages of the manuscript on which they were working so that he could examine them. Unforgettable and unrepeatable, the congeniality in which she worked with him. And I still see, for example, the great happiness of the two of them the evening after they finished his book on Anselm, which Karl always regarded as his greatest, as we sat out in the garden enjoying Mozart's music and Ruedi's splendid wine, amid the larkspur and the fragrance of the phlox. An unforgettable picture of the two in their oneness of intellectual communion.[6]

The intellectual and cultural liveliness and openness of the thirties were reflected in the evening gatherings at Bergli.[7] The friends who gathered so happily took turns in writing poems, making up stories, or playing charades. "Karl's products, especially his poems, were real works of art, . . . Lollo's were tender and aesthetic."[8] Gerty Pestalozzi had many cultural interests and was often the initiator of playful discussions of such themes as astrology, organic health measures, and the like.[9]

The women who gathered every year at Bergli found a bond in, among many other things, the women's movement.[10] It is likely that Charlotte first came into contact with the questions and problems of women's liberation at the college for women she

Bergli, a Place of Shared Work

6. With Karl Barth in the study at Bergli.

attended in Berlin.[11] She later became deeply involved in the questions of the role of women in the church and in society and also immersed herself in the writings of Simone de Beauvoir.

In the years that followed, she and Barth returned again and again to the undisturbed work at Bergli.

In the meantime Charlotte had through her own studies increasingly qualified as Barth's co-worker in theology. He had become convinced more and more that she was now indispensable to him, and he invited her to go to Münster and from then on to live at his side as his co-worker.[12]

6
Time Together, Work Together

On October 14, 1929,[1] Charlotte von Kirschbaum moved into the Barth family home in Münster. "At that time those who were involved had no idea what they were letting themselves in for."[2]

Barth had issued this invitation because he had discovered in her a "fellow spirit,"[3] a woman who shared his burning interest in the theological issues of the time. He invited her to share his life in order to make their work together more productive and intensive, but also because she had become a close and trusted companion. Beyond their theological work the two were united by a "deep mutual attraction."[4]

> Yes, he had found in her a helper who had the staying power to follow him on the long, distinctive road he was traveling, one who not only accompanied him but in her own way shaped him—a woman who became for him in his searching and development, in his encounters and debates, but also in his times of quiet rest from his work, a helpful and trusted partner.[5]

Charlotte von Kirschbaum gladly accepted this invitation—"she took her happiness into her own hands"[6] but it was also for her a great risk, because "she placed herself in an extremely unprotected position."[7] This step resulted in a final break with her

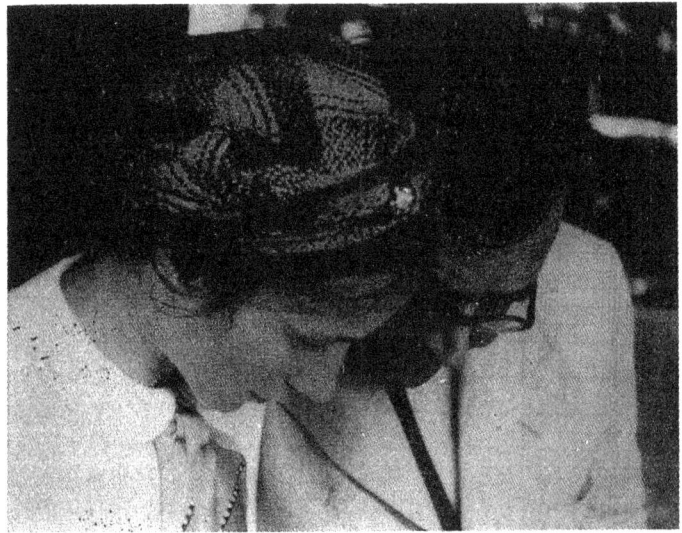

7. Working together.

mother. Nor were her brothers willing or able to understand this decision for her life, and from then on her name was hardly mentioned in the circle of her acquaintances.[8] She, however, made efforts to maintain her contact with her family.[9] Even Barth's mother was offended by the presence of Charlotte von Kirschbaum in her son's life, and good friends turned away from him.[10] Georg Merz regretted to the end of his life that he had introduced them to each other.[11]

Life in the Barth household became difficult and full of stress for everyone. Certainly it was a bitter experience for Mrs. Nelly Barth to be confronted daily by a woman who shared much more of her husband's world than she could, for as a careful housewife she was fully occupied with caring for their many guests and with the upbringing of their five children. For her the "intimate presence" of Charlotte von Kirschbaum with her husband demanded an unwelcome "hard renunciation."[12] She lived more and more in the background. "But for all that she did not let her husband go."[13] They both held fast to their marriage. "She too sought in her own manner to follow him on his ongoing way."[14] She too performed in her own way "work in the shadows," for without the work she carried out in the background as housewife and mother, the intensive work done by Barth and Charlotte is hard to imagine, and "they were both aware of that."[15]

"Barth did not hesitate to take on himself the responsibility and guilt for the situation that had resulted. But there was, as he saw it, nothing that could be done. The situation had to be accepted and borne with by all three of them."[16] Everyone suffered in this stressful life, not least the Barth children. Each of them too had to come to terms in his or her own way with the difficulties in their parents' house. It must be noted, though, that Charlotte von Kirschbaum was loved and cherished[17] by some of the children as "Aunt Lollo." "We must remember too that in the following eventful decades the three also had to struggle to display dignified endurance and tolerance of this burden and these tensions."[18] Charlotte became a full member of the family: a situation "desired by him, tolerated by Nelly, and by Lollo passionately accepted."[19]

7
A Suitable Counterpart and Helper

Entry into the Barth home meant for Charlotte von Kirschbaum, in addition to the personal burdens, that from then on she was engaged in strenuous work in the Barth style, from "early morning until often late in the evening, interrupted only by a short pause at noon with black coffee and a game of cards for diversion."[1]

During the winter semester 1929–30, Barth was dean of the theological faculty in Münster, and in a letter to Thurneysen on November 16, 1929, he described their work. Charlotte was in charge of the typewriter and "is busy from early until late with the business of the dean's office, with the preparation of the scholarly references that lie behind my lectures and then form the basis of my writings, and with her own reading and the reports she makes on them. I often wonder how I was ever able to get along without her."[2] Not only was she involved with the assembling of the reading matter for his lectures and seminars, she was always present at them. In addition, she studied Latin with Barth's daughter Fränzeli three times a week "in order to be able to get acquainted with the Reformers and Church Fathers in the original texts,"[3] which she was soon able to do.

In December 1929, Barth made the acquaintance of the philosopher Heinrich Scholz. Their discussions were often mediated by Charlotte von Kirschbaum. Each day she attended Scholz's lectures on Kant and, as Barth put it, "afterward over coffee and cakes she had to talk with him for at least an hour."[4] Following that, she reported to Barth on what she had learned. Scholz was quite taken with this intelligent and beautiful woman, fell head over heels in love with her, and even made her a proposal of marriage.[5] This proposal was no temptation for Charlotte.[6] She neither could nor would give up theology, and she had determined to continue along the road on which she had set out with Karl Barth, no matter how difficult it might become.

Charlotte von Kirschbaum was not only a helper for Barth but also a "counterpart," a "self-reliant partner, fully his equal."[7] They "stood together face to face"[8] or, as Barth's daughter-in-law Rose Marie put it, "vis-à-vis."[9] She relieved him of a great part of his work by helping with the preparation of his class lectures, his essays, and his public speeches, in that she followed the daily newspapers and the newest publications in theological journals and reported to him on them. She also assumed responsibility for part of his correspondence. All this took place with Barth's full agreement, and he placed complete trust in her. "From the thirties on she was to the public the 'voice of Karl Barth.'"[10]

In addition she was his primary partner in discussion. With her he could think through and discuss all his new theological reflections and developments, and her contributions were certainly not without influence on him. In their exchanges of ideas she often corrected one-sided tendencies, and through the variety of their reflections she enriched his thought. Her advice helped him in both larger and smaller decisions that had to be made.[11] Charlotte understood Karl Barth as no other person did. This is what made the help she gave him as his "partner" distinctive.[12] "By this [the strength of her under-

8. Charlotte in 1929.

standing] she helped him, gave him support, and day by day gave him courage and joy,"[13] and "it might even be said that the great significance that Eduard Thurneysen had for Karl Barth in the early years now became her lot."[14]

There was only one respect in which she was not his equal—she had no independent means. Like his family she lived on his income. As Barth's life partner she had "whenever she wished or needed it complete access to the money in the house"[15] and received in addition about a hundred marks in pocket money each month.[16] Thus she was assured of everything she needed. She received no financial remuneration for her scholarly work. Charlotte von Kirschbaum did not have an employer-employee relationship with Karl Barth.

The financial independence on which we women today place great emphasis as the basis for a relationship of equality did not seem important to her.

9. Traveling together.

She was well provided for, had everything she needed, and that seemed to satisfy her.

In the years that followed, Charlotte accompanied Barth on almost all his travels.[17] And in March 1930 there was no question but that she would go along to Bonn when Barth was called there to the chair of systematic theology.

8
Confessing the Faith in the Church's Struggle

Because Charlotte von Kirschbaum accompanied Barth whenever he taught, she came in close contact with his students, both male and female. She was psychologically more sophisticated than he was, and again and again she opened the way for students to have access to him.[1] At that time in Bonn the closer circle of his students included Georg Eichholz, Walther Fürst, Helmut Gollwitzer, Heinz Kloppenburg, Werner Koch, Walter Kreck, the student adviser Erica Küppers, Georg Lanzenstiel, Lili Simon, Karl Gerhard Steck, and Hellmut Traub.[2] Among them she made many good friends, and these friendships continued even after the years in Bonn. During the years of the church's struggle she kept up her correspondence with Helmut Gollwitzer and Erica Küppers, for example, and thus they gave her support and companionship in this difficult time. Indeed, Gollwitzer continued to be a person to whom Charlotte von Kirschbaum could turn for support throughout her life.

It is not surprising that Barth's students respected this extremely attractive and intelligent woman, and many "worshiped at her feet."[3] She was someone with whom they could talk about their personal problems, and often she helped them by providing them with a book now and then or slipping them some money.[4] Theology students were regularly guests at the noon meal in the Barth household. In her contacts with Barth's students and assistants, Charlotte von Kirschbaum was probably a stricter "Barthian" that Barth himself. She was more radical and unconditional and watched out to make sure that the Barth theological line was maintained.[5]

It was with increasing concern that Charlotte followed the political events of these years, the growing strength of the National Socialists and the increasing threat to democracy. "Her departure from Munich had not least of all a political significance. With this step she abandoned Georg Merz, who was becoming more and more nationalistic and conservative, and joined herself to Karl Barth, the Social Democrat."[6]

In the following years she stood fully with Barth, supported him, and shared his decisions. A significant indication of this is that she became a candidate of a third party in the church elections, the party "For the Freedom of the Gospel," an alternative to the slates of the "German Christians" and the Young Reformation Movement. This general election of the Evangelical Churches was held on July 23, 1933. In Bonn, Charlotte's party won 10 percent of the vote, so she was among those elected to the governing body of the Bonn parish.[7]

Early in 1933, Barth had already started to form a Confessing Community among the Protestants in Bonn and had written a declaration, the so-called "Bonn Theses," which later served him as a draft for the Theological Declaration of Barmen. Even though years later Charlotte von Kirschbaum no longer remembered these theses,[8] we know from the research that Christoph Barth did into the history of the Barmen Declaration that she was familiar with them. Christoph Barth established that his father had dictated the theses to the typist before he threw his handwritten manuscript into the wastepaper basket, from which his son later retrieved it.[9]

Charlotte took part in person at the meeting of the Reformed Synod in Barmen on January 4, 1934,[10] and she continued to follow the development of the Barmen Declaration at first hand. Concerning the meeting of the committee of three in Frankfurt, May 15–16, 1934, about which Barth informed her, she wrote in her diary, "In Frankfurt, good work together with Asmussen and Thomas Breit—Sasse was sick. Confession formulated with full agreement."[11] Moreover, the "Basel manuscript," the oldest copy of the texts drafted in Frankfurt and edited by Barth, contains Charlotte von Kirschbaum's handwritten comment in the margin, *Barmen Declaration 1934—original.*[12] All these activities show that she took part in the development of this document.

We may assume that she accompanied Barth on a number of his journeys to lecture during this stormy time of debate within the church in Germany. On January 23, 1934, she attended a gathering of church leaders and theologians, at which it was arranged for representatives of the two church camps to have an audience with Hitler.[13] Later, when they were back in Switzerland, she accompanied Barth to Germany for his last lecture in Barmen, October 7, 1937, on the topic "Gospel and Law." Barth was not permitted to deliver the lecture himself, and the manuscript was read by Pastor Karl Immer. The evening of that same day the police placed the two of them on a night train and escorted them to the border.[14]

It required courage in those years to accompany Karl Barth and to stand by him so staunchly, years in which step by step he was driven from his professorship in Bonn, out of the Confessing Church, and out of Germany, because on the basis of his theological statements and his resulting political stand he was no longer acceptable to the National Socialist State or to the Confessing Church.[15] In a letter to their friend Erica Küppers, Charlotte told of Barth's refusal to take the oath of allegiance to Hitler, unless he could add the words "in so far as I can responsibly do so as an Evangelical Christian," and of the disciplinary action that followed.

She wrote:

This event [the disciplinary action] is of profound significance and perhaps even sets a precedent for the recent development of the Confessing Church. Karl can only be a disturber of a church led by such as [Bishop] Marahrens. ... That it is not possible to explain Karl's motives clearly to everyone, or perhaps only to a few, Erica, is something that we must be content to accept. That a few do understand is shown by the many letters that have come in these days. ...

Yes, the road ahead is now very dark for the Confessing Church. The path of least resistance brings a peace of sorts. But, Erica, the efforts of these years to shake people awake was not useless. A marvelous letter from Niemöller [November 26, 1934] says the same. The whole issue now is simply a revival of the old church, which, however, the way it is now, has no future. We must have patience and know how to wait. I am sure that this is not the end. ... That Karl had to act as he did is now very clear to me, and that is a comfort even with all its consequences.[16]

9

Committed Service in Swiss Exile

On June 22, 1935, Karl Barth was abruptly placed on retired status by Bernhard Rust, Minister for Cultural Affairs. This was done in spite of the fact that a ruling by the court in Cologne on December 1934 relieving Barth of his teaching position had been rescinded. Charlotte von Kirschbaum had handled most of the correspondence with Barth's friend, the lawyer Otto Bleibtreu, which had secured the rescission.[1] Since even the Confessing Church was reluctant to give Barth a teaching position in theology, he accepted only a few days later a call to Basel. In the meantime Charlotte had long since made all the necessary preparations for their departure.[2] She and the Barth family left on July 6, 1935, for Basel, where they moved into the dwelling at 186 St. Albanring.

In Switzerland, Charlotte continued to follow the events in Germany and to help wherever she could. Together with Barth she worked with the Swiss Society for Aid to the Confessing Church, which was organized in Zurich on January 5, 1938.[3] This society enabled pastors and pastors' wives exhausted by their work in the Confessing Church to have a time of rest in Switzerland, provided for "the distribution of pamphlets and leaflets, including some by Barth," and concentrated its efforts later on helping Jews and Jewish Christians who were expelled from the Third Reich.[4]

In addition to these activities, those years were marked by an exceedingly great amount of work: on the one hand, work involved in Barth's teaching at the University of Basel and his work on the *Church Dogmatics* and, on the other, extensive travel to lecture in Switzerland and abroad, all of which required preparation and research. In both areas Charlotte shared the work, as Barth's partner in discussions and in the process of thinking through and developing his writings, which she edited and typed. In addition it was important, especially in those times, to maintain contact with German friends. Here too she relieved Barth of much work by organizing his correspondence and, in complete intellectual agreement with him, carrying on part of it herself.[5] Thus it is not surprising that in these perilous times Dietrich Bonhoeffer often directed his letters to Charlotte and that she was the one who answered them.

Bonhoeffer had planned to visit Barth in May 1942, but he often heard that Barth was suspicious of Bonhoeffer's time in Switzerland "because of the commissions entrusted to him."[6] Many in Switzerland had come to distrust Bonhoeffer and to wonder how it was possible in the middle of the war for him to get passport, visas, and Swiss currency for his trips to Switzerland. What services was he performing, in whose name, and for what purpose? In a letter to Barth he attempted to learn for himself whether Barth really mistrusted him; if that were the case, he would prefer not to visit, even though that would be a painful decision. The answer to his letter came from Charlotte von Kirschbaum, who replied by return mail that Barth was "breathlessly awaiting his colleague."[7] With this letter she relieved his doubts; Barth approved of his visit and was looking forward

10. Charlotte in Basel, 1943, age 44.

to it.⁸ But even so she gave him quite openly to know that Barth mistrusted and opposed an eventual coup d'état by Prussian generals for which Bonhoeffer would do the fetching and carrying.⁹

This exchange of correspondence between Charlotte von Kirschbaum and Dietrich Bonhoeffer was unexpectedly brought to light in 1981. Clearly, it is extremely significant and can contribute to a better understanding of the relationship between Barth and Bonhoeffer.¹⁰

In 1943 a highly dangerous incident occurred. Charlotte's German passport had expired (to the end of her life she remained a German citizen), and in order to renew it she went to see the officials of the German embassy in Bern. Not only was her passport not renewed, they demanded that she surrender it. Losing her passport would have resulted in deportation to Germany, in those years a sentence of death. Alert to the danger facing her, she stubbornly refused to hand over her passport, and the following day it was renewed. Dr. Hans Bernd Gisevius, a member of the German resistance movement around generals Beck and Oster, was vice-consul in Zurich and took care of the matter for her.¹¹

10
Toward a Free and Independent Germany

In Zurich in August 1943, in response to an initiative of German Communist émigrés interned in Gordola, Switzerland, the Movement for a Free Germany was founded. The stimulus for this action was a radio broadcast that told of the establishment of a National Committee for a Free Germany in the vicinity of Moscow. There German emigrants and prisoners of war from a variety of social backgrounds and political positions had come together to form a "united committee to struggle against the Fascist war effort and to seek for ways to establish a free, independent Germany."[1]

Since the formation of such a committee was not permitted in the Swiss internment camps, a group met in the Zurich cantonal theater under the leadership of Wolfgang Langhoff (author of the song "Die Moorsoldaten") and founded a local chapter. They immediately began publishing a journal, *Freies Deutschland,* and other literature.[2] Soon men and women of greatly differing political beliefs joined the movement, and branches were founded in several Swiss cities, including one in Basel in 1944 that had the support of Karl Barth.[3]

These local branches suggested the formation of a nationwide organization, embracing members of the various political parties and representatives of the churches. At first the national leadership could only be provisional, and officers could not be chosen, as the Committee for a Free Germany was still illegal in Switzerland. Otto Salomon, who had been suggested as the representative of the Confessing Church, did not want this office, because as a member of the Ecumenical Council of Churches he had "strict orders" to "refrain from any 'one-sided' political activity which would violate the police regulations governing the activities of foreigners and thus jeopardize his work permit."[4] Charlotte von Kirschbaum then declared that she was ready to join the provisional leadership as representative of the Confessing Church of Germany.

Meetings were held secretly in a back room of a restaurant near the Rhine bridge in Basel.[5] The provisional leaders included six Communists, two Social Democrats, one Democrat, and a representative of the Confessing Church.[6] They viewed their task as coordinating the various branches, providing publicity, and working for better conditions in the internment camps. The first conference of the Committee for a Free Germany took place January 27–28, 1945, in Zurich, and its first concern was the legalization of the movement in Switzerland.[7] In March of the same year the Swiss government recognized the movement and gave official permission for the publication of its journal.

Thus at the second national conference, on May 27, which Karl Barth attended as a visitor, new leadership could be chosen. Together with Wilhelm Abegg, the former Prussian Secretary of State, and Wolfgang Langhoff, Charlotte von Kirschbaum was chosen as a member of the leadership council.[8] She held this office until the dissolution of the Committee on December 16, 1945, on the grounds that there was no longer any need for political activities in exile.

Karl Barth felt very close to this committee. It interceded for improving the status of émigrés, through numerous publications and lectures in-

11. With leadership council members Wolfgang Langhoff and Wilhelm Abegg (at lecturn).

formed the Swiss about the political situation in Germany, engaged in the tasks of unity, reconstruction, and reparations, and worked for the formation of a free democratic Germany.[9] In February 1945, Barth made it possible for the members of the committee to meet with Protestant émigrés in his house. He reported on this meeting in a letter: "Unfortunately the Christian émigrés did not show up well in contrast to the much greater simplicity and the goodwill of the others, who claimed to be atheists but in reality reacted in a much more Christian manner."[10] In his opinion Charlotte von Kirschbaum understood "how to get along extraordinarily well with the Reds and the Reddish."[11]

Even the attempt to deport Charlotte to Germany,

which fortunately did not succeed, did not scare her away from political activity. Nor, unlike many others, was she shy about working together with Communists in a cause she believed in.

11
An Immeasurable Contribution

In the midst of the varied tasks and projects of those times, Karl Barth had begun in 1931 the writing of his *Church Dogmatics*. He set himself the task of setting forth in a multivolume work the doctrine of the word of God, of God, of the creation, of reconciliation, and of redemption. This task occupied him—and kept him going—until long after his retirement in 1961, and yet even so it remained unfinished. In the course of the years the work grew to thirteen volumes and a total of 9,185 pages. For the completion of the fifth and last part, "The Doctrine of Redemption," Barth, now at an advanced age, lacked the strength. This powerful opus could have been accomplished only through strenuous, concentrated work. Moreover, this work, in its vast extent, was possible only through the work which Charlotte von Kirschbaum "quietly accomplished" at Karl Barth's side.[1]

She relieved him of many tasks and thus, to a certain extent, kept his hands free for this major creation. As we saw in the Introduction, Barth himself wrote that, beyond all this, "she has devoted no less of her life and powers to the growth of this work"[2] than he himself. "Without her co-operation it could not have been advanced from day to day, and I should hardly dare contemplate the future which may yet remain to me."[3] She made an immeasurable contribution to the origin and the continuation of the work on the *Church Dogmatics*.[4]

Karl Kupisch, who allotted barely a half page in his biography of Barth to Charlotte von Kirschbaum, described their shared work as teamwork.[5] He goes on to say that "she knew how to watch over at the side of the master, knowledgeably, and with a firm hand and steady zeal, the direction and the progress of the gigantic work that was developing."[6]

In my estimation these remarks show clearly that her share in the work on the *Church Dogmatics* was not limited to the typing and editing of his manuscripts, work she accomplished in addition to her other duties. Barth's choice of words implies a much more extensive contribution.

As already noted, Charlotte took charge of the file of quotations, made excerpts from theological readings, read the works of the Reformers and Church Fathers, and gathered their most important citations "into Barth's barn." This defined the way in which her collaboration in the development of the *Church Dogmatics* took shape. That is, she took over the preliminary work of preparing the excurses on matters of exegesis[7] and historical theology. In this way "her immeasurable share in the origin and further development" of this gigantic work, also found its way into the sections in fine print. The compilation of such comprehensive excurses as are found throughout the *Church Dogmatics* was an extremely time-consuming task that Barth would never have been able to carry out alone. It is work that could only have been performed in harmony and accord with Barth's own thought. Unerringly she recognized related—and also foreign—thoughts and concepts and knew how to introduce them at the right places, a sure indication of profound acquaintance with the material and its theological and philosophical relevance.

It was Barth's style of work, in discussion with a

"partner," to try out his theological reflections and newly won insights, to develop them further, and to expand them. He also entrusted to those who worked with him their own areas of work in full confidence that they would act responsibly.[8] We can be sure that Charlotte von Kirschbaum's preliminary work was discussed between the two of them and only then incorporated into the *Church Dogmatics*. " 'These parenthetical passages' [especially the exegetical ones] were so important to Barth that he sometimes wondered whether he should not have reversed the order and printed them in large print and his own explanations in fine print."[9]

In 1956 Charlotte von Kirschbaum and Ernst Wolf edited the *Festschrift* for Karl Barth's seventieth birthday under the title *Antwort*. This volume includes a bibliography of Barth's writings and publications from 1906 to 1955, which she compiled.[10] She also facilitated for Barth's readers an overview of and access to his works by preparing the helpful indices to each individual volume of the *Dogmatics*.

Along with the many and varied responsibilities that Charlotte von Kirschbaum had assumed and carried through effectively, she found, amazingly enough, sufficient time to enter into the debate over a theme that was near to her heart. Quite early she had become deeply interested in the women's movement, and she was especially concerned with the position of women in society and in the church. She directed her attention especially to the works of Simone de Beauvoir and corresponded with her.[11] She differentiated her position from the existential position of de Beauvoir and endeavored to develop an "Evangelical doctrine of the role of women."[12]

Her starting point was the Bible. She made a careful exegesis of those texts of the Old and New Testaments that contain stories about women or that deal with the position of women. As a result she followed a middle ground between de Beauvoir on the one

12. Outside the Barth house in the Pilgerstrasse, Basel, 1948.

hand and, on the other, the Catholic mariology of Gertrud von Le Fort. She presented the results of her study publicly for the first time in four lectures, which she delivered in the spring of 1949 in Bièvres, France.[13] She revised these four presentations and in September 1949 published them in book form with the title *Die wirkliche Frau* ("The Real Woman").

In the years that followed, she continued to lecture on this theme: in spring 1950 in Geneva on the writings of de Beauvoir; in 1951 in Basel on "The Role of Women in the Proclamation of the Word"; during the winter of 1953–54 in Hamburg and in Mulheim in the Ruhr on the biblical view of women; and in 1960 she prepared to undertake a new lecture tour in Germany.[14]

12
Charlotte von Kirschbaum— *"Die wirkliche Frau"?*

In Charlotte von Kirschbaum's book, which she saw as a first step toward a Protestant theology of women,[1] she explores the position of women in a doctrine of creation.

If we seek to place her teaching in the context of Karl Barth's christocentric theology, we can say that her starting point is the "final instance" of the analogical schema of Barth's thought. According to Barth's doctrine of election, the heart of his theology, the triune God, who in himself is not lonely but is in relationship, created the world out of pure grace to be his creaturely counterpart. God decreed that the second way of being, the Son, should become a human being. Thereby Jesus Christ is *the* chosen human in an absolute sense, the *imago dei* of the trinitarian God, who is in relationship. Therefore Jesus Christ must be a relational being—the Christian community constitutes his counterpart. Therefore, humans who know that they are chosen through Jesus Christ live in relationship. The *imago dei* in human beings consists in that each of them exists as a human in relationship with other humans. The relational existence of humans is manifest in their nature as sexual beings, male and female.

Charlotte von Kirschbaum's reflections and explorations begin at this point, the relationship between men and women, and in this way she carries forward, to a certain extent, Barth's theology.

Eberhard Busch has written as follows about Charlotte von Kirschbaum's work: "For quite some time she had been deeply concerned with the issues in this area. A part of her research and its results had already been quietly incorporated into the *Church Dogmatics* III 2."[2] A comparison of what she wrote in the first three chapters of her book with paragraph 43:3, "Humanity as Likeness and Hope," in that section of the *Dogmatics*, reveals obvious parallels in content.[3]

Her thoughts, her statements about the position of women, reveal throughout the marks of autobiography. In many places her interpretation of biblical texts lets us hear clearly the voice of the author and gives expression to her own life experiences. Thus her book is interesting not only as a continuation of Barthian theology, and as a theological debate about the relationship between the sexes from a woman's point of view, but because it gives insight into Charlotte's own understanding of her relationship to Karl Barth. It can be regarded as her "scholarly based self-confession," her "statement of accountability before God and man."[4]

In the early chapters of her book, in which she presents her basic thoughts on the position of women, Charlotte von Kirschbaum begins with the biblical accounts of creation as the foundation for the equality of the responsibility and the equality of the grace received by man and woman. God did not create human beings for loneliness but in a duality of man and woman, the basic form of human existence. Thus the loving encounter between man and woman, the encounter between an "I" and a "Thou," is a unity willed by God. Nonetheless, within this relationship of man and woman the woman has a distinctive position. She was placed at man's side as a helper, a counterpart (see Gen. 2:18), and thus is in a position subordinate to his. But in Charlotte von Kirschbaum's interpretation this does not mean that the woman is in any way inferior. A relationship between man and woman in which each in his or her own position affirms the other in love is a parable of the relationship between Jesus Christ and his church (see Eph. 5:22–33). The subordinate position of the woman in her relationship to the man is a parable and a reflection of her Christian position in relationship to Christ, and thus the woman represents the Christian community. This is her special distinction and duty; by her natural subordination she is witness and example for the church, which subordinates itself to Jesus Christ as its Lord.

"It is not good that the man should be alone; I will make him a helper fit for him" [German: *ein Gegenüber*, a counterpart]. This Bible passage assumes a central place in her book. Again and again she turns to it in order to clarify the relationship between man and woman. The strong emphasis on these Old Testament words is not accidental; rather, it expresses in clear language Charlotte von Kirschbaum's understanding of her relationship to Karl Barth.

Those who knew Charlotte von Kirschbaum well characterized her as a "counterpart" to Karl Barth. As a partner equal to him in birth, equal in quality, who was made subordinate to him as his helper—that is how she understood herself and how she structured her life at Karl Barth's side. She lived and worked totally for the life work of this one person. As his helper she worked quietly, in obscurity, and it is there that she has been left by the subsequent writing of church history.

The relationship God wills for man and woman is established at the individual level through marriage. "The *total* person seeks here the *total* person. A merely partial affirmation runs the risk of unfaithfulness."[5] In her clear and unambiguous manner Charlotte von Kirschbaum never accepted a "both-and relationship" between man and woman. For her there was only an either-or, a yes or a no.

Charlotte had respect for Barth's marriage, even when the interrelationship of these three persons often made daily life unspeakably difficult. But she had decided to be there for only this one man and to accompany him in her way, as his counterpart. Thus she could say that the question of who it would be that wished to realize in marriage the unity of man and woman which God desires is "a question of a person's situation and destiny, and ultimately of providence. . . . And it may well be that it is the unmarried man or woman who lives stronger in encounters than many a man or woman in marriage."[6]

Charlotte von Kirschbaum found a distinctive role for women not only in the position of a symbol and model for the Christian community but also in the motherhood of Mary. Mary, as the mother of Christ, fulfilled the hopes and longings of the mothers of the Old Testament, hopes that were directed toward the son who would be the Messiah of his people.[7]

> Mary was privileged to be the first to experience the incarnation of the Son of God, experiencing it in her own body. Herein lies the greatest distinction that a woman can receive. World history may ascribe to men the deeds of history, but the history of Jesus Christ is no history of men! At the birth of the Lord man was missing. Mary is the *virgin* mother.[8]

Still, she rejected any elevation of Mary "as a symbol that had become a gestalt, that is, as an eternal truth about humans that had become a gestalt,"[9] as we see her presented in the mariology of the Catholic theologian Gertrud von Le Fort.[10] Since it pleased God to become a human being in the womb of a woman, Mary may therefore rightly be called "Mother of God," but "her mission in its uniqueness is a definitely limited mission."[11]

But Charlotte von Kirschbaum was not limited to

talking about biological mothers in the Bible. She also cited the passage in Isaiah 54:1, which says, "Sing, O barren one, who did not bear; break forth into singing and cry aloud, you who have not been in travail! For the children of the desolate one will be more than the children of her that is married, says the LORD." From this she concludes that "there is therefore a motherly existence which excels biological motherhood. There are prophetic women who become spiritual mothers."[12] As examples of such mothers she mentions Deborah, Zipporah, Abigail, and Huldah.[13]

Indeed, it was not only students of Karl Barth but many others to whom Charlotte von Kirschbaum was devoted, especially during the Hitler period, who came to know and treasure the maternal side of this woman.

In the final chapter of her book, where she ventures some "critical evaluations," she distinguishes between the Catholic view of women held by Gertrud von Le Fort and the existentialist position of Simone de Beauvoir. She shares to a large extent the latter's analysis of the situation of women but is no longer able to agree with her when she states that the "sexual differentiation of male and female is not an essential feature of their existence in the world,"[14] that the division of individuals into male and female is not their final destiny. "On the contrary, the biblical testimony is that in actuality humans were created as man and woman, the basic forms of human existence. . . . Their sexual differentiation . . . is therefore the primary feature of their existence."[15]

A further distinction from the existentialist position lay for Charlotte von Kirschbaum in the differing understandings of freedom. While the existentialists begin with the assumption that nothing can make a person free except the person himself or herself, the Bible testifies "that persons can live as 'liberated' because they *are* liberated. They do not

13. At Le Croisie, April 1950.

move toward that goal, but move forward from that goal."[16]

Her book, which lets the reader see clearly the theologian Charlotte von Kirschbaum, is also at the same time a distinctive document for a deeper understanding of this person, for a deeper understanding of her decision to lead her life at the side of the famous theologian in spite of all difficulties. *Die wirkliche Frau* appeared also in Japanese in 1956.[17]

Her doctrine of the position of women, which she herself characterized in the foreword to her book as only a "rough draft," is clearly to be understood and evaluated in terms of the times in which it was written, even if women in the church of today would hardly defend it any longer as "doctrine." We should approach critically the position she held on the basis of her strong emphasis on the biblical and theological teaching that men and women belong together: namely, the position that excludes the possibility of a homosexual relationship as a freely chosen way of life. Still, it should be noted here that both she and Karl Barth included in their circle of friends a number of homosexuals.[18]

Her book can be understood as a step toward the reading and interpretation of the Bible from the point of view of women, as preparation for theological debate over the position and status of women in society and in the church. Her foreword ends with the words, "May others who are better able than I take up and advance this cause."[19] In the past twenty years, despite opponents who accuse them of heresy, women in the churches have devoted themselves to this task, have come to new conclusions, and have courageously taken further steps forward.

13
As Her Strength Failed

Charlotte von Kirschbaum's last major journey took her to the United States at Karl Barth's side in 1962. Accompanied by Barth's sons Christoph and Markus they traveled through the vast breadth of that land, pausing at various places for lectures, meetings, and sightseeing.[1]

In that year she began to show the first signs of an illness which, in the years that followed, increasingly took control of her. Those who were close to her observed a strange decline in her competence. She was known to everyone for her organizational talent in keeping the calendar of Barth's engagements and as his "business manager,"[2] but now she forgot deadlines and appointments and mislaid important papers.[3]

In addition she had been suffering for some time from being unable to sleep uninterruptedly or even at all. She could not make up for the sleep lost at night, important as it was to do so, because her heavy daily work load allowed her no time for an afternoon nap. The loss of sleep and the resulting fatigue rendered her illness worse,[4] and soon a rapid decline of her mental powers became apparent. Because she was energetic and goal-oriented she attempted to continue to work at the same tempo, and she also tried to encourage Barth, who in the meantime had begun to tire easily, to get more sleep and to persevere in his work.

In a letter to Helmut Gollwitzer on May 31, 1962, Barth wrote, "Naturally you, like so many others—including Lollo—urge me to resume work on the *Church Dogmatics* with even more energy."[5] Barth wondered whether there was any point in adding a thirteenth and a fourteenth volume to the twelve volumes of the *Dogmatics,* or whether he should not leave that to others. "What if I have not already had my time. . . . Lollo cannot bear to hear me express such thoughts. She will fume when she reads this, will berate me as an old reprobate, and if possible will try to keep this letter from being mailed."[6]

It is probably more than chance that Karl Barth broke off his work on the *Dogmatics* when the progress of Charlotte von Kirschbaum's illness made it increasingly difficult for her to continue working with him.

The awareness that she was slowly but surely losing her memory, which was often also Karl Barth's memory, and her ability to think clearly, led her close to despair, and at times this almost reached crisis proportions.[7]

By the end of 1965 her decline was so far advanced that she needed continuous nursing. In order to see that she had proper care, she was moved in early January 1966 to Sonnenhalde Sanatorium near Basel. After this, Eberhard Busch, then still a student and assistant to Barth, took over a part of her responsibilities.[8]

In the last analysis it is not possible to determine what led to this early onset of illness. Was it the extremely great mental effort that had been demanded of her since the thirties? Was it caused by the heavy work schedule, which we today can hardly even imagine, but which confronted her daily and drained her powers almost to the point of exhaus-

14. Sonnenhalde Sanatorium, near Basel.

As Her Strength Failed

tion? Or were the tensions in the Barth household, which she had had to contend with day after day, finally more than she could bear? We may surmise that each of these factors played a greater or lesser role in her premature decline.

"Mercifully Lollo is somehow spared from having to experience the burden of her condition,[9]" Barth reported to Helmut Gollwitzer in a letter. In his final circular letter after his eighty-second birthday in May 1968, Barth gave those who had sent congratulatory messages a report on the condition of Charlotte von Kirschbaum:

> An especially positive feature of my personal life is the hour which I spend every Sunday with my beloved Lollo von Kirschbaum at her Sonnenhalde in Riehen. Without her commitment and hard work the entire middle period of my life and work would have been unthinkable. Now, as a result of her illness, it is as if what she once was is now covered with a veil. But the good Sisters there tell me she is a patient that they like to care for. And what did she herself say to me just two weeks ago? "Everything is so difficult and so beautiful, and that way it is also more interesting!" And, when we parted, "My, we have it so good!" ... Even in her feebleness she is an inspiration to me.[10]

On his visits to her, on which he was accompanied either by Pastor Martin Schwarz or by his son-in-law, Max Zellweger-Barth, it was Barth's custom to sing chorales for her, and she, rousing slightly, would respond to them.

14
"A Long, Slow Departure"

"Karl Barth entrusted to his son-in-law the complete care of Charlotte von Kirschbaum, and he, after Barth's death on December 10, 1968 . . . visited her at least once a week. Mrs. Nelly Barth and the members of her family also visited the patient from time to time. And her relatives and friends in Germany were faithful in their concern for her."[1]

"It gave her great pleasure if a visitor brought a doll and amused her by joining her in play."[2] Was playing with dolls a sign of second childhood or the expression of a wish for children that had remained unfulfilled? In the course of time she lost her ability to speak, and only sometimes when someone called out to her a well-known name did she respond with a look of recognition in her eyes.[3]

Always one year older than the century, she finally died on July 24, 1975, six and a half years after Barth's death. "It was a long, slow departure"[4] that extended over more than ten years. "The long years in the nursing home were more and more years of sleeping, always moving farther away."[5] It was an unusually "long-drawn-out departure, but for her, thank God, less painful"[6] than for all those who were close to her and shared the experience of her slow but inexorable decline.

Charlotte von Kirschbaum was buried July 28, 1975, in the Hörnli cemetery in Basel. Following

Barth's wish, and with the agreement of Mrs. Nelly Barth,[7] for whom life together with Charlotte had not been easy to bear, Charlotte von Kirschbaum was buried in the Barth family grave. Nelly Barth found there one year later her own final resting place.

The sermon at Charlotte von Kirschbaum's funeral was given by her long-time friend Helmut Gollwitzer. "Among the funeral guests were the then president of the Federal Republic of Germany, Dr. Gustav Heinemann, and his wife."[8] In the sermon, Gollwitzer directed the following words to the mourners:

"The way that the new life in us is always struggling against the forces of death was experienced in the destiny that was Lollo's in the circle of Karl Barth, destiny now not in the heathen but in the Christian understanding of this word—a providence in the happiness and pain and tasks, often all-too-difficult tasks that were her lot, a providence which no one could or should escape who in responsibility sought to be obedient to it, each of you in his or her own way, and which no one could escape without experiencing mutual hurt and guilt, guilt which brought all of us the experience that the life which is ours through the death of our Lord Jesus Christ comes to us as forgiveness. To you who were most involved, it was granted by this forgiveness to give thanks for this providence. This you were able to learn again and again, and even these last ten years during which Lollo was withdrawing were a help in learning it."[9]

This providence, as Helmut Gollwitzer formulated it, which brought Charlotte von Kirschbaum to Karl Barth's side, shaped her life, a life that was dedicated totally to one person and to the service of his creativity: the life of a self-assured woman, who felt called to accompany Karl Barth as his counterpart, and who did not let the resulting heavy tasks and bur-

15. The Barth family grave in Hörnli cemetery, Basel.

dens turn her from her course; the life of a woman who, because of her life decision, was attacked and treated with painful contempt and who, after her death, people were glad to quietly forget. It is difficult to comprehend that the life of this woman and her constructive theological accomplishments at the side of the world-famous Karl Barth have remained in obscurity so long.

Lectures by
Charlotte von Kirschbaum

Address for the Movement "Free Germany"
(Delivered in St. Gallen, Geneva, and Montreux, 1945)

What do "Confessing Church" and "Free Germany" have to do with each other? Why are we Protestants also in this movement, especially since we are Christians fully committed to the Protestant cause? Does the church have anything at all to do with politics? Isn't it the church's sole responsibility to proclaim the gospel: that is, the good news of the victory of Jesus Christ and the claims of the kingdom of God? Isn't the church subject to the Lord's words, "My kingdom is not of this world"?

Yes, it is the task of the church, the task of the local congregation in the world, that it proclaim this kingdom of Christ. In recent centuries the church has been a little forgetful of this task. It has proclaimed other messages and announced other kingdoms. I am thinking for example of the kingdom of culture and of science, and also of that fateful kingdom of German nationalism, which reigned in the church long before Hitler. Then came the year 1933 when this cozy relationship between church and world was suddenly disrupted because the National Socialist state reached out for the church, as it did for all areas of life, in order to force it into the service of the state. It wanted the church to "conform," just as the schools, the courts, the universities, and everything else had been made to "conform."

And then the unexpected occurred. The church

defended itself against this attack. There were those in the church who not only bowed to the state but joyfully accepted its demands, the so-called "German Christians," who now proclaimed from their pulpits the splendors of the Third Reich and the revelation that had been given to the German people through Adolf Hitler. That they also used extremely rough methods served to make many circles in the church draw back and defend themselves against this imposed conformity. But these wide circles, the so-called center of the church, did not really abandon the ground on which the traditional church had been standing; that is to say, they did not revise the previous cozy relationship with the world and with the state, but were simply in style and were unwilling to go along with the crude falsifications of Christian doctrine. If these circles, and they included the so-called leaders of the church, had only resisted there would have been no need to speak of a church struggle. This old church would have quickly enough been left aside by the National Socialists as quite harmless. And that is what they did.

But then in addition to the German half-Christians and this middle group there were Protestant congregations and pastors who, through the attacks of the Nazi state on the church, were led to a basic reflection on the nature and the mission of the Protestant church These congregations and pastors came together to form synods and to hold congregational retreats, and they united in their confession of their Lord Jesus Christ, whom alone they would obey and whom alone they would proclaim. Thus the Confessing Church came into being. For this confession did not remain mere lip service but strove to find expression in all areas in which the church operates.

I am not going to talk to you tonight about the details of the German church struggle. You are certainly aware of them, at least in part. It was essentially a defensive struggle. The church wherever possible resisted the attacks of the Nazi state on its realm; it fought for the purity of its witness, its teaching ministry, its organizational structure, and its leadership. And so it came to pass that in the midst of the triumph of the injustice and violence which the Nazi regime in Germany represents, the good news was still proclaimed. This proclamation did not directly involve the political events of the time, however, and many have criticized the Confessing Church for, so to speak, defending only its own interests and not carrying its efforts beyond the walls of the church.

Indeed, we confront here a boundary of the German church struggle. But it must not be forgotten that the churches in Germany were in reality the only places where there was organized opposition to National Socialism. The brave resistance of innumerable individuals from other areas of society are also recognized. But if only all these other areas and institutions had defended their own concerns, things would be very different in Germany today. Having established this, we must admit that the Confessing Church, not out of a lack of courage but from a lack of insight, acted too timidly in defending and emphasizing the ecclesiastical nature of its struggle. It was of the opinion that church and politics have nothing to do with each other, and that the church would be denying its "proper task," which it had now finally begun to take seriously, if it involved itself directly in the issues of the state. An investigation of the causes of this attitude of the Confessing Church would lead us too far afield. I will only remind us that it was above all Lutheran doctrine which was receptive to such a separation of the two realms.

It was others who were called on to continue the struggle. As a resistance movement formed in the countries under Nazi occupation it was the churches of these lands that worked with these movements, often in positions of leadership. In Holland, Norway, and Denmark, in France and in Czechoslovakia, Protestant and Catholic Christians took an active part in the struggle of their people. They did not do so by denying their duty and responsibility as the church but, rather, by recognizing that their confession of Jesus Christ as their only Lord had to be made real beyond the boundaries of the church in this fight for justice and freedom. "All authority in heaven and on earth has been given to me" was a message to be proclaimed by deeds of active resistance to all powers that were gathering their strength to threaten this Lordship. These churches would not have been able to carry on their struggle if the German church had not already focused on that which is entrusted to the church, if it had not launched its defensive struggle against the temptations and threats of National Socialism. These other churches carried on the struggle in a legitimate manner; they bore testimony to the sole Lordship of Jesus Christ over his church and his sole Lordship over the world.

Today we confront the collapse of our German people. We are at the end. Twelve years of Nazi power have proved enough to make Germany, outwardly and inwardly, a heap of rubble. We are laden with guilt and shame like that of no nation before us. How can we even dare to speak of a "Free Germany"? Is this not merely a new motto on our lips, a promise we cannot keep?

We must honestly admit that it is a promise. We are still standing at the beginning of a road whose end we cannot foresee. But we German men and women who have gathered here in the movement Free Germany in Switzerland are committed to traveling that road. Not because we have found some new password and now instead of saying Heil Hitler! we are to say Heil Stalin! or Heil Churchill! but because we are one in the belief that we no longer have any other choice than to take together, *united*, the next necessary steps. This is our last chance. We stand together in the knowledge that we share the guilt of the immeasurable misery which Hitler has brought on our people and on the entire world. That is no pious statement, but a sober conclusion. None of us were able to prevent this disaster, we were unable to prevent the rise of National Socialism in Germany, and we were unable to break its power. To do that required the overwhelming force of arms, the airplanes and tanks of the Allies.

Do we want to say that it is not a general German guilt? Do we want to be exceptions as those who "never joined in"? Do we want to demonstrate again that we are an immature people and are not capable of bearing the responsibility for our political life? Because we are resolved to take on ourselves this responsibility for today and tomorrow, we also voluntarily take it for yesterday and confess that we too, where we were, did not do all we could. I have endeavored to show how the Protestant church, with its timid holding back from all politics, did not carry out as well as it should have its role as watchdog. Similar statements could be made about all the responsibilities of the church, and I myself have heard from the mouth of a leading Communist that his party often admits that it is guilty of not being able to unite the labor movement and thus form a block in opposition to the Nazis. Anyone who today seeks to be excused from this guilt would not really be ready to make a new beginning but would only be ready, in the church or in politics, to maintain connections with yesterday. This new beginning is manifest in that we leave the old quarrels behind us, and that Germans of all groups and levels of society who are persons of goodwill unite in a common effort to make a new beginning.

I am often asked by Christians how I can justify working together with Communists. I can only answer that the Communists in our movement have proven to be responsible and to be as greatly concerned about the future of Germany as we are. In this connection, let me read a letter from a Communist friend in Würtemberg who until recently was a leader in our movement.

Our friends do not always have the right attitude toward the occupation forces. They complain about occasional excesses, and they are surprised that the army of occupation does not act forcefully against the Nazis, because they expected that the anti-Fascists would now have everything the way they wanted it. But then these friends reflect, Who was it who did what it was our job to do, the difficult task of freeing us from the Nazis and the Gestapo? The Allies did the biggest job. Everything else is now up to us. If the occupation armies had wanted revenge they could have acted much differently from the way they do. It is my perception that the French are behaving very well. Things have become more relaxed over the weeks that have passed. Now our people must really prove themselves. . . . When we see things in the larger context and do not get hung up on isolated events, we can be happy, especially as our friends are finding success if they move out of their passivity and do practical work. Everything depends on such activity.

Who can deny that these words express a loyal attitude toward the Western occupying powers and are by no means an attempt to play off the Russians against them? These Communists know as well as we do that the future, not only of Germany but of all Europe, depends on peace between West and East, and that it only serves the interests of the Nazis and all other destructive elements to sow the seeds of discord. No, we stand together with the Communists in our movement in a shared and honorable responsibility. Christians who feel anxiety here should ask themselves the question that a Communist recently posed to me: "Why is it that you Christians are afraid of us? If you were sure of your own cause you wouldn't be anxious."

In this shared work we are not under any illusions, but recognize this work on German soil as the path that we now must follow. In recent weeks we have received confirmation of this in letters received from a pastor in South Germany, who is seeking in his community and in his congregation to work for reconstruction in the sense that we mean here. He had received the recent pamphlets by Professor K. Barth, which some of you may also have read. He writes:

> Yes, how can the Germans become healthy and how can the world become healthy, because both are sick? I am now working to answer your question as it apples to the German people in the present moment. Those outside Germany must think that among us a very radical rejection of Hitler and his system has taken place or is taking place. And it is also true that after the "Hosannas" come now the cries of "Crucify," but no one will admit having been present, and all without exception wash their hands in innocence. It is one of the saddest chapters in our history and casts a dark shadow on the character of our people, that after having cherished that system, not one person among us stands up as a martyr for his convictions. People are ready today to raise a new flag and to march behind it with new ideals. But the frightening thing is that I very seldom find genuine repentance and submission under the terrible guilt which we have brought on ourselves and under the unspeakable misery that together and separately we have caused through Hitlerism. Even among those who would be Christians I very seldom find it. No one should be deceived. If Hitler came back and began again to be victorious, and raised the rations of meat

and bread to the peace-time level, our poor, erring people would again shout his praises. As long as Hitler was successful, that is, until about the time of Stalingrad, this people followed him and dreamed with him the frenzy of future glory and world power. Only when the tide turned and we no longer could live on the goods and the labor force of other nations, but more or less had to provide for our own needs, did the falling away begin until today this falling away has reached the stage of disgust with Hitler and his accomplices. But this disgust lacks any shock over that which took place through us and which must now be made good.

And what we see on the faces of our people is actually more annoyance that things turned out badly than an inner renunciation of the methods of brutality, force, lawlessness, and contempt for human life and freedom. What is now needed is that our people be summoned unceasingly to to true repentance, first before God, and then before man, so that they may be terrified by the abyss that opened up in their souls. This must primarily be the task of the German churches. For this purpose, however, we must have solid factual material at hand. The greater proportion of our people unfortunately do not know, or have only hints of what has happened. But only against the background of this reality which cries out to Heaven can our people be told in concrete terms what it is of which they must repent and from which they must turn away forever if they are to live and not just vegetate, if they are to find their way back into the community of free peoples. General calls to repentance will be answered with the comment that other peoples have not done much better or acted more honorably. Thus enlightenment on a grand scale must take place in order for the work of opening people's eyes and re-educating them can take place.

You can see that behind these words there are no illusions about our people, but there is the honest will to begin once more in hope, a new beginning for our people. The following lines may show how difficult this is:

> Unfortunately we have no newspapers to disseminate to our people the most necessary items of information about the events in the past and in the present. Except for church gatherings no other public assemblies are permitted; there is no paper that we can use to mimeograph important expressions of opinion, no mail and no telephone service so that we can stay in touch with our nearest colleagues. Thus it is hard to form enlightened public opinion. But it must and will be done. This gloomy picture would show you the situation, except for a few hopeful bright spots that I want to show you. It moved us deeply and showed us how close we still are to each other when you wrote that real Communists visit your study. The same has happened here. In the early days after the arrival of the Allied troops a few committed Communists came to see me, because they simply felt the need to be with other persons who had not sold out and to discuss the situation with them. And since then they have come to see me from time to time. We know that despite all the differences between our respective starting points we are in agreement with them and see the necessity to stand together with all those who have not drunk from the cup of wrath, and to do that which lies at hand to do. It is a hopeful sign when church people and Communists can leave the old stereotypes behind them and deal with one another as one responsible human being to another. Perhaps we can hope for something new to come from this. We can learn from those Communists who are now traveling the same road with us something of activity and discipline. In any case

there are here among then quite a few persons who are truly intelligent and worthy of our respect. Perhaps they will be the means by which we can set our lame fellow-citizens in motion.

You see that the way ahead is hard; it is more than that. At the same time we heard from a social worker who works in the same community and was a member of our Free Germany movement here, that this region of Württemberg—the district of Rottweil, which has no rural areas—is experiencing widespread hunger. The weekly ration is one pound of bread, supplemented every four weeks by 200 grams of meat and 200 grams of butter, and nothing else. But here too the most recent reports are that through the cooperation between the pastor, the mayor, and the social worker the worst danger has passed, and through conscientious distribution at least the minimum for subsistence has been made available. This cooperation won the trust of the army of occupation, so that some measures have been relaxed.

Such small steps as this are the beginnings of reconstruction. And by such small steps we here in Switzerland, who in spite of everything still have it so much better, must begin. We do not have a grandiose program to offer you and no suggestions for administering a program. We wish only to make a new beginning. We can only appeal to you to join in and to do the next thing that you find to do to lessen the difficulties and the great feelings of hopelessness that the German people confront. You know that there is a Swiss Committee for Aid to Germany, and that here many measures are being planned. But it is essential that we Germans living abroad take the initiative ourselves in coming to the aid of our fellow countrymen. Thus the movement Free Germany has in recent weeks begun its own program of assistance to coordinate efforts, including the work here in

Basel. One particular program has been established to care for the most urgent needs of women and small children in Germany. Last night I heard the report of a church official who had just returned from Germany and who described for us the unimaginable misery that women in Germany are now suffering. He emphasized again and again how urgent is the need and how important it is that concrete steps be taken to provide specific aid. Since the help that we can provide is quite limited, we have committed ourselves to the concrete step of concentrating on aid to the district of Rottweil, because we have specific reports from there and we can maintain regular contact with them. We can be assured that the distribution of our gifts will be in good hands and that through our gifts we can provide support for brave men and women, support that has an inner value that is no less than its material value.

I want to ask all the women here tonight, if at all possible, to join in our group here in Basel that will provide help for women. No one will be excluded who wants to share in our plan for sewing and mending used clothing that we can make serviceable again. Tomorrow night there will be held in our offices at 20 Imbergässlein a discussion to which you are all invited. In addition, Mrs. Strenz will be happy to provide information for you here this evening.

"Confessing Church" and "Free Germany." Have we abandoned our theme and ended up in a sewing and mending circle? No, it is in such little things as this that we can show that we understand our shared responsibility; that such little things cannot be separated from larger, ultimate matters; that we Christians are concerned for the world, and this means not least of all that we are concerned for the poor and the lost. But can there be a greater poverty and a greater lostness than that of our people today? To help this people today does not mean to go blindly about doing good from some spontaneous warmth of heart; it means making this people once again responsible for their own lives, to free them slowly from the terrible dependence and blindness into which their blind leaders of the blind have led them. The movement Free Germany is dedicated to this purpose. Can we Christians hold back from this service? Can we say it doesn't concern us? I am afraid that if that is our response we have understood little of the gospel, and our confession of faith means little.

The Role of Women in the Proclamation of the Word

(Delivered in Basel, 1951)

In the report on "The Life and Work of Women in the Church," issued by the first assembly of the World Council of Churches in Amsterdam in 1948 and containing research material from the churches in fifty-eight countries, there is the remarkable conclusion that this study uncovered reactions that were typical of each of the denominational traditions. Thus in general the Congregationalists, the Quakers, and the Salvation Army—that is, churches and societies in which the congregation is the source of all ministry—are quite open to dealing with this question, since they "have a clear conscience. They have complete equality of offices and professional status for men and women." They encounter problems in practical questions, but "their standpoint is clear in reference to that which they regard as the teaching and example of Christ" (p. 7). The report goes on to say that it is the churches in the Anglican tradition, especially in England, who are the most negative on the question of the position and activity of women. They reach differing conclusions, "but on one point they are unanimous: that is, that women cannot be ordained" (p. 8). In the churches of the Reformation, however, which stand in the middle between these two extremes of left and right, there is great uncertainty over the participation of women in the work of the church. In part we find—according to the report—"a not insignificant rigidity" on this question, but on the other hand there is a remarkable flexibility that can possibly be traced to the Reformation understanding of the "priesthood of all believers." In general, however, we find these churches, Lutheran as well as Reformed, in a state of confusion over the position of women in the church, especially in reference to their service in the proclamation of the word. It is here that the problem first truly becomes a theological problem. May women participate actively in the proclamation of the gospel in the worship of the congregation? In Lutheran terms, are they permitted to exercise the "spiritual office"? During the war years in Germany a very objective and thorough investigation of this question was made by a study group commissioned by the Confessing Church. A collection of the historical and exegetical materials produced by this group is available in a mimeographed report [edited by Dr. Hennelies Schulte], which shows how seriously the leading German theologians, both men and women, wrestled with this problem.

If we leave aside the various irrelevant arguments that have been raised against the participation of women in the proclamation of the word, there remain two questions that we must take seriously:

I. Does the New Testament contain an authoritarian concept of church office which as such excludes the participation of women?

II. Does the Pauline statement about the subordinate position of women prohibit their participation in the proclamation of the word?

I

Under the old covenant in Israel there was an office to which only men were called, the priestly office. Access to the Holy of Holies in the Temple was open only to priests. A priest mediated between God and the people when he presented the sin offering at the altar. After Jesus Christ has brought reconciliation once for all, a priestly office in the Old Testament sense cannot exist any longer. (On what follows, compare Eduard Schweizer, *Das Leben des Herrn in der Gemeinde und ihren Diensten,* 1946.) Now everyone in the congregation has access to the sanctuary, now all are taught by God (1 Thess. 4:9), now all are spiritual (Gal. 6:1). But only Jesus Christ is the high priest (Heb. 7:26–29), and in such a way that he is also the sacrifice of reconciliation. A bloodless repetition of the sacrifice on Golgotha in the sacrament of the altar—as the Catholic sacrifice of the mass is intended (significantly there is therefore in the Roman Catholic Church still a sacramentally consecrated office of priest to which only males can be called!)—cannot be found in the New Testament. "But you are a chosen race, a royal priesthood" is addressed to the entire congregation (1 Pet. 2:9).

Jesus Christ alone is the office bearer, the liturgist. The term which the Septuagint uses for the priestly office, *leiturgia,* is, with two exceptions (Rom. 15:16; Phil. 2:17), used in the New Testament only of Christ. The work of the congregation is termed *diakonia,* service. All human activity can only be service in the activities of the Lord. *Diakonia* in ordinary Greek usage means serving those at table (as it is also in Luke 17:8; John 12:2; and Luke 12:37; cf. Luke 8:1–3; 10:40; 22:26) and thus is an insignificant and humble rendering of service. The content given to this term in the New Testament is something new. In contrast to Greek and pagan thought, which always gave a low estimate to service and regarded the master who was being served as higher in rank than the servant, a reevaluation took place. "But I am among you as one who serves" (Luke 22: 27). These are the words of the one who is Lord of the Kingdom. Jesus Christ is not only the office bearer, the liturgist, he is also the servant, the *diakonos.*

Therefore his disciples are told to accept for themselves this reevaluation, this new order which was established by their Lord. "Whoever would be great among you must be your servant, and whoever would be first among you must be slave of all. For the Son of man also came not to be served but to serve, and to give his life as a ransom for many" (Mark 10:43b–45). This path from above downward is an absolute contrast to the natural human way of life. It is the Kingdom of God, which, still hidden, breaks into the world in this way. To complete this movement, or to put it in different terms, following the Lord on this path means that it will be necessary to suffer in this world. It involves service to the point of sacrificing one's life. "If any one serves me, he must follow me" (John 12:26). It is those who are his, who are called by the Lord to this living community of the Holy Spirit, who are his followers. It is the communion of saints to whom this service is committed. It is "the act that proceeds from the inmost heart of God, in the carrying out of which it comes about that specific persons in the midst of the activities of the world know this, and in their words and works, in their activity and suffering, they can confess that which is real for the entire world, but which the rest of the world does not yet recognize, that which through them is to be communicated to the rest of the world—that Jesus Christ is Lord" (Karl Barth, *Theological Studies,* 22, p. 25). Christians serve their Lord by serving one another. Submission to his lordship is expressed concretely in submission to one another. "As each has received a gift, employ it for one another, as good stewards of God's varied grace" (1 Pet. 4:10). It is the gift of the exalted Lord through his Holy Spirit which makes this service possible and which forms its basis. The one who really exercises these gifts of grace is the Lord himself. He gives to the members of his body a share in these gifts (cf. Rom. 12:3; 1 Cor. 11:19; 12:7; Eph. 4:7). Not every member of his body receives the same gift, but each one the gift that is his or hers, and each, with that gift, is necessary for the service in the community. "The parts of the body which seem to be weaker are indispensable," says Paul (1 Cor. 12:22). They all need one another, all serve the building up of the body of Christ. Nothing is said in this context of a difference between the sexes. Both men and women are called to service in the church. "I will pour out my Spirit upon all flesh, and your sons and your daughters shall prophesy" (Acts 2:17). Here they are all one in Christ Jesus, and there is neither male nor female (Gal. 3:28).

There is, though, one special office, that of apostle. It is listed first among the gifts of grace mentioned by Paul (1 Cor. 12:28; see also Eph. 4:11). But this "first" said of the apostles is not only first in time but also is distinct in nature. An apostle is an eyewitness of the risen Lord and was given his office directly by the Lord. "That which was from the beginning, which we have heard, which we have seen with our eyes, which we have looked upon and touched with our hands" (1 John 1:1). "Am I not an apostle? Have I not seen Jesus our Lord?" Paul asks (1 Cor. 9:1). He was called by a special appearance of the risen Lord, like "one untimely born" and "last of all." With his call, according to the New Testament, the direct calls through the risen Lord came to an end. From then on all service can only be service through the word of these first witnesses, the repetition of the apostolic kerygma. The Lord rules his community through this word and his Holy Spirit. "He who hears you hears me" (Luke 10:16).

This distinctive and singular position of the apostles in the church and in contrast to the church finds a correspondence (which is significant for our problem) in the fact that the circle of the apostles was exclusively male, that it included no women. We should not here appeal to the women to whom the risen Lord appeared on Easter morning. To be sure he appeared first to women (according to Matt. 28:9–10, to several; according to John 20:14–17, only to Mary Magdalene) and commissioned them to go to the brethren and tell them that they had seen the Lord. This encounter and this commission are beyond doubt a distinctive experience, but it is a distinctive singling out of members of the community from among Israel who follow the Lord; it is as the first of the chosen people that these women are honored. This did not lead to their inclusion in the number of the apostles. The task committed to them was limited by time and by its content. It was carried out and thus it is also completed. The proclamation of the one who was crucified and is now risen was not carried by these women beyond the borders of Israel out into the heathen world; that was done by the apostles whom the Lord sent, and whom he prepared for that task by breathing on them and saying, "Receive the Holy Spirit" (John 20:22). They were to be his messengers and the bearers of the testimony that calls the community into life, which the community can only hand on, and which it can only obey.

Thus the contrast between apostles and community is not continued by a contrast between "office" and community. The entire service of the community, including the service of offering the gospel through word and sacrament, is subject to the apostolic kerygma. Paul does indeed mention the kerygmatic gifts and ministries first, and we cannot deny that they hold a central place, but basically he does not distinguish between them and the other forms of ministry (Rom. 12:6–8; 1 Cor. 12:28; see also Eph. 4:11). Thus there should be no question but that from the very beginning there were orderly and permanent ministries in the church, but only such that were a part of the total ministry of the church. The church as a whole is the bearer of these ministries, it receives the authority to call the various members, and thereby it takes on responsibility for these members in reference to their outward existence. The church can in response to this call and commission only be obedient to the call of the Lord; that is, it can only acknowledge the gifts which the Lord has given to each of his servants. This acknowledgment is itself a gift, and thus the call is a charismatic act of the church in prayer. Through its own decision it can only serve the decision made by its Lord.

Here we must at least note that there is in the New Testament a line of tradition that places more emphasis on the "offices" than we find in the letters of Paul (see Eduard Schweizer, *Die Gemeinde im Neuen Testament,* Theologische Studien 23, and "Die Urchristenheit als ökumenische Gemeinschaft" in *Evangelische Theologie,* 1950, p. 273). In the church in Jerusalem, as generally in the Palestinian churches, Jewish forms lived on, and there was a marked difference between these churches, with their "official" nature, and the churches founded by Paul. Thus we may ask whether the earliest church did not have a concept of church that differed from that we find in 1 Corinthians 12 and 14. The question is drawn more sharply in reference to the post-Pauline churches. As the Pastoral Letters show, they had clearly become more rigid in their forms and had "conformed to the world." The charismatic gifts, which, as Paul shows, cannot be confined and limited, seem here to have become confined to institutional limits, and there is a question as to whether it is really the gifts of grace that are the basis of service here, or the "office" that guarantees the gifts of grace. Thus Timothy is exhorted, "Do not neglect the gift you have, which was given you by prophetic utterance when the elders laid their hands upon you" (1 Tim. 4:14). Or "I remind you to rekindle the gift of God that is within you through the laying on of my hands" (2 Tim. 1:6). Here the Roman Catholic concept of the sacramental consecration of priests, which confers this authority, seems to continue the priestly office of Christ and thus is no longer far removed from the concept of a habitual grace. But we must be careful not to forget that even in the Pastorals it is not an office or an official that is the "pillar and bulwark of the truth" (1 Tim. 3:15; See Schweizer, *Gemeinde nach dem Neuen Testament,* p. 18).

The authority of Timothy and Titus—the individuals to whom these letters were addressed—is subordinate to that of the apostle. They act as his agents; they do not have the authority to begin something but are to "continue in what you have learned" (2 Tim. 3:14). Thus their work is incorporated into the total ministry of the church, and their advantage over the other servants of the church is limited to the fact that they were called directly by the apostle and commissioned by him. He commits specific authority to them, such as installing presbyters and teachers, but this derived authority does not place them in the distinctive relationship that the apostle has to the community but, rather, empowers them as prominent members of the community to perform their ministry of the word, to which they, together with all the other members, are subject.

It would then be a misreading of the two lines of tradition in the New Testament if we were to construct from the Synoptics, the book of Acts, and the Pastorals a "Jewish church of official positions" and to contrast it with the "fanatic spiritual church" of Paul. For Paul, the victory achieved through the death and resurrection of Jesus Christ was the "turning of the times" in a manner quite different from that which the earliest church thought, and therefore for him the break with the past had to be carried out in a much more radical manner. But this does not mean that the tradition was not still alive for Paul too, or that he did not also know of a regulated order and discipline for the church. He warned the church in Corinth of the danger of a fanatic understanding of their Christian freedom and pointed them to the message of the cross and also to the obedience that the church must display as it waits during the time between the resurrection and the return of its Lord. The kingdom of God has not yet arrived, we still live by faith and not by sight, and the building up of the church is still not complete. But on the other hand the earliest church is not simply a continuation of Jewish ecclesiastical order. The spirit living in the church is the spirit of the new covenant, and the knowledge of the fight Jesus wages against all the forces of authority is absolutely clear in the words transmitted by Matthew, "But you are not to be called rabbi, for you have one teacher, and you are all brethren" (Matt. 23:8). Thus here too there is no office that is not ministry and service.

The contrast between the officers and the members of the church, which has increased more and more even in the Evangelical churches, is foreign to the New Testament, for the New Testament knows of no distinction between "spiritual leaders" and "laity" in the church. "You are all spiritual." Even the communities that, in contrast to those founded by Paul, still had Jewish tendencies or already had catholicizing tendencies, knew this.

Thus, for example, a concept like that of A.F.C. Vilmar can scarcely find any basis in the New Testament (see Vilmar, *Dogmatik,* 1874, p. 275). He concludes from article 5 of the Augsburg Confession that "for the formation of faith it is necessary to have a special office instituted [by God], and also the faith and salvation of the congregation: that is, the continuing existence of the church is dependent on the presence of this office, so that the congregation is constituted and preserved through the ecclesiastical ministry. The congregation has and possesses nothing and gives itself nothing of this salvation but is always in a position of receiving"—not, we should note, from the Holy Spirit but from this "office" that transmits itself from person to person, and does so "through the laying on of hands, which as the transmission of the direct mandate of Christ bestows the Holy Spirit in full reality." "In the spiritual office Christ is the judge of the world, and according to their relation to those who hold this office the masses will one day be judged, as we see in Matthew, chapters 16 and 25" (*Dogmatik,* vol. 2, p. 322). But according to Vilmar this office—in distinction to Catholic doctrine—is not derived from the apostolate but rather "arose under the same through the ordinances of the Apostles as specially instituted by Christ" (ibid., p. 274).

Vilmar puts forth here an interpretation of the Lutheran confessions that can hardly be in agreement with their intention. The Lutheran confessions acknowledge a "spiritual office," which as such is committed to the entire community. The "keys" belong not to specific persons but to the church, and there is no intermediary. The community calls specific persons from among its members, and it is God who through the mouth of human beings makes the decision. The recognition of the charismatic gifts of the members and thus the call they have from God is a gift of grace, and the call through the congregation is therefore a charismatic act. In this sense ordination can be termed a sacramental act ("Apology for the Augsburg Confession," XIII, pp. 12–13). This "spiritual office" is ordered by God for all times and all peoples and is thus founded on divine authority. On the other hand, the concrete shape of the office (since the "spiritual office" as such is real only in connection with other functions) is here and now, based on the decision of the congregation and therefore based on human authority. The freedom of the believing community, in obedience to divine authority, allows the church from time to time to establish ecclesiastical rules and to alter existing ones. Thus the question of whether a woman can be called to the office of the proclamation of the word—that is, the preaching office—is not to be answered in the negative on the basis of *jure divino* but to be left open, and, even according to the Lutheran understanding of the office, judgment is to be reserved to the community.

In theory the Reformed position presents no difficulties for the participation of women. There is nothing here of a spiritual "office" in the sense in which the term is used in the Lutheran confessions. Calvin, as is well known, recognized four offices: teachers, pastors, presbyters, and deacons. "Proper order is observed . . . when all, with no exception, heed Christ as the highest king, when they are led by his Spirit, and the church shows itself to be his body, the community of the Holy Spirit, in which all members serve one another according to the gift that has been given to each." That is Calvin's position (Niesel, *Die Theologie Calvins*, p. 191). Unfortunately, we must say that in practice, even in Reformed circles, one encounters an inappropriate stubbornness in reference to the participation of women in the proclamation of the word. (Highly instructive in this connection is the debate among Gertrud Herrmann, Pastor D. Wilhelm Rolfhaus, and Karl Barth under the title "Ungehorsam gegen Gottes Gebot?" ["Disobedience to God's Commandment?"] and "Der Schrift Gehorsam" ["Obedient to Scripture"] in the *Reformierte Kirchenzeitung*, 1932, nos. 25, 28, 30.)

From the preceding discussion we may conclude

that on the basis of the New Testament no understanding of an authoritarian "office" can be derived that would exclude in principle the participation of women. In the New Testament, "office" is termed *diakonia*. And to this all who are members of the body of Christ are called, each with the gift that he or she has received. The singling out of one of these services in the sense of the Old Testament priesthood is possible only where this service lays claim to the authority of a mediation between God and the community. To do this, however, is to approach too closely to the authority of Jesus Christ and to recognize with the Roman Catholic Church the continuation of the priesthood of Christ, without being able to share the Roman Catholic understanding of the sacrament. The central meaning of the service of proclaiming the word can really only come into full play where it involves in truth the service of the word; that is, where the Lord himself acknowledges the word of the preacher and through the power of the Holy Spirit makes it into the word of God. That is the miracle by which the community, and the one who ministers through the divine word, live. The servant of the word does not possess the grace, but it must always be bestowed on the servant anew. Where that is acknowledged, the "office bearer" will let go of all accumulated authority and stretch out his or her hands to receive this gift, which alone can authorize anyone and which makes the service of the proclamation of the gospel in itself "miraculous."

II

The instructions of Paul to the Corinthians seem to stand like a threatening prohibition over the entrance of women into the ministry of the proclamation of the word: "As in all the churches of the saints, the women should keep silence in the churches. For they are not permitted to speak, but should be subordinate, as even the law says. If there is anything they desire to know, let them ask their husbands at home. For it is shameful for a woman to speak in church" (1 Cor. 14:33b–35).

Paul clearly bases this instruction not on an authoritarian concept of office (these words stand at the conclusion of his remarks about the gifts and the ministries based on them), but on the position and function of women.

It will be helpful to begin by recalling the concrete context in which these words were written. Paul is speaking about the order of the worship in the congregation in Corinth, an intellectually rich and "gifted" church (see 1 Cor. 1:4–5). But now it is precisely this richness that poses a threat to this congregation and might well lead it into a fanatical self-understanding. The Corinthians are in danger of misunderstanding the freedom that is now theirs in Christ. They believe they are in control and can decide for themselves what authority they will submit themselves to. They are "puffed up" (4:6,8; 5:2) and act as if they had not received everything that is theirs. This shows clearly that they are "of the flesh" in their way of thinking, for all their spiritual riches. By wanting to reject the authority of the apostle Paul, and with it the authority of the word, they are losing the unity that is given through the word alone. Quarreling and jealousy are breaking out in their midst. Paul reminds them that he became their "father in Christ Jesus through the gospel" (4:15). He urges them to imitate him and together with him to submit themselves to the word of the cross, which, in their fanatical anticipation of the kingdom of God, they think they can ignore. According to Heinrich Schlier (*Evangelische Theologie,* 1949, p. 462), it is possible to regard the relationship between gnosis and agape, knowledge and love, as the major concern of First Corinthians. And Adolf Schlatter holds that the letter has only a single theme: namely, "the foundation of the apostolic authority, which the church cannot reject" (see *Paulus, Der Bote Jesu,* 1934, p. 5). These two positions are not mutually contradictory but are thoroughly in agreement in substance. In the specific examination of the passage that concerns us here, we can say that the focus of chapters 12—14 is the relationship between charisma and ministry. The tension in this relationship becomes especially acute in the gatherings of the congregation for worship. The enthusiasm of the Corinthians brings the goal of their worship—the edification of the community—into question. They were not seeking to serve this goal with their gifts, but to indulge themselves in ecstasy. There are some who speak in tongues, even when there is no interpretation to make what they say understandable. Some are prophets who prophesy even when their voices are drowned out by other prophets, so that what they say cannot be heard by the whole congregation, and thus it is not possible for others to "learn and all be encouraged" (1 Cor. 14:31). Here we are dealing with the gifts of the Holy Spirit, but clearly these gifts can be misused by those who receive them and thus be used for fanatical self-gratification rather than to serve the community. "Let all things be done for edification" (v. 26). If this goal is lost sight of, the spirits of the prophets are no longer subject to the prophets, and everything will be in disorder. But "God is not a God of confusion but of peace" (v. 32). The community can be built up only through the knowledge based in love, and thus only through the charisma that serves the Lord and his church, not oneself.

Paul knows that women, like men, receive the gifts of the Holy Spirit in the community and also the kerygmatic gifts. In 1 Corinthians 11:5 we have specific instructions for the behavior of the women who serve through the proclamation of the word. No woman may prophesy or pray with her head uncovered, but she should cover her head so that in this ministry also she should remember that she is functioning as a woman, and that she should not belie her position. In this context we are not concerned with the often-discussed question of the contradictions between 14:34 and 11:5–6. (See my book, *Die wirkliche Frau*, p. 48.) Rather, we are concerned with the fact that in both passages Paul is above all concerned that in worship women should be aware of their responsibility as women. Clearly the apostle regards this ministry as indispensable in its role in building up the community.

Thus the differentiation between the position of men and women in the church—that is, in the place where two or three are gathered in the name of the Lord, and he is present in their midst—is not irrelevant, not abolished in an equality that wipes out this distinction. The words of Paul in Galatians 3:28 are not to be understood in that way. The unity in which "there is neither male nor female; for you are all one in Christ Jesus" does not mean that individuals cease to be what they are but that in spite of this they are taken up equally into this unity as God's children. It is as such that they will recognize the special responsibility which is demanded of them as man or as woman. And now it is the responsibility of the woman that especially interests the apostle in this context of the worship of the church. He outlines the order in which men and women are placed together and states, "the head of a woman is her husband" (1 Cor. 11:3). The person who is designated as the "head" takes the leading position in that particular group. He is in a position superior to the other partner or partners and takes precedence over them. In our case, the other partner is the woman. And when Paul instructs women to be subject, he is telling them to recognize and accept the position that has been accorded to them. This is what "irritates" us. Does this mean that even Paul, as a child of his time, regarded women as inferior creatures who had to submit to the leadership of men? This is a false conclusion that cannot be avoided if we understand these words in isolation and not in the context of Paul's thought. For Paul, the position of women is by no means inferior to that of men. This is shown by the fact that the sentence "the head of a woman is her husband" is found in a parenthetical passage that is usually read and interpreted by exegetes with much shaking of heads.

Thus for example, Hans Lietzmann (*An die Korinther I, II,* in the *Handbuch zum Neuen Testament,* 1931, p. 53) says, "The dominant thoughts in the following explanation (vs. 3ff.) are not entirely intelligible to us. . . . We cannot understand why Paul did not omit v. 3 with its forced play on words (vs. 4–5) and in both cases simply appeal to the generally accepted custom." Bousset (in *Schriften des Neuen Testaments,* 3rd ed., p. 128) writes, "It is not clear what Paul's purpose is in this remark, which moreover subordinates women to men in a manner that does not agree, for example, with his freer opinion in Gal. 3:28." And Bousset concludes with the question of whether perhaps v. 3 might not be "a remark written in the margin at a later time."

Paul inserts the anthropological statement about men and women in two sentences about Christ, which cast light both on the place of men as well as on that of women. He begins, "The head of every man is Christ," and he concludes, "the head of Christ is God" (1 Cor. 11:3a). Christ is in both the superior position and in the inferior; yes, he is both the one placed above and the one placed below. He is the Lord and the servant as the one who was crucified and is risen again, the King of his kingdom, and as the one who was crucified and rose again, he is the one who harkens to the will of his Father. Paul by no means intends here, as many think, to describe a series of differing ranks (God, Christ, man, woman), as a result of which the man would have direct access to Christ but the woman would have access only mediated by the man. Rather than that, he is depicting the independent and direct relationship of each in his or her place and his or her position. The position of both men and women is sanctified in that Jesus Christ chose them both, and therefore the promise and the commands of Christ are for both.

In the light of this equality of birth every evaluation of one's position is baseless, and each one as a being created by God can only recognize and accept in thankfulness the lot in life which God has prepared. "Just as it is with other things, so too it does not stand within anyone's power to be man or woman. The sun cannot say, I will be the moon, and neither can the moon act as if it were the sun, but each must remain as it was created by God" (Luther, "Sermons on the First Book of Moses," Weimar ed., 24, 52). That I am a man or a woman is a part of the fact that I have only one life, which lies determined in the will of the Creator. God's command calls me to recognize God's will, including his will for my sexual identity. This places a claim on me, and whatever else it may mean, man and woman, each as such, is claimed by God, each in his or her own place; this is the basis for the independent responsibility of each as the counterpart of the other. That the man is the "head," that he goes first, but the woman follows, that he calls, but the woman answers, can only mean that he is called upon first to watch over the system in which they are placed with each other. He is always tempted to misuse the power, the *exusia*, that is entrusted to him within the relationship of being a counterpart. He definitely is not to "rule" over the woman. We all know that the words people appeal to so often, "he shall rule over you" (Gen. 3:16), were spoken for the relationship under the old covenant, a relationship broken by sin, and therefore they should be quoted (in either marriage ceremonies or liturgies!) only in the sense in which they are interpreted in the New Testament: that is, in the light of the order restored in Jesus Christ and his church. In this new order the man is not commanded to "rule" but to "love" (Eph. 5:25), and the woman, in accordance with her original destiny (Gen. 2:18), to be a help to him as his counterpart. That is her share of the responsibility for the created order which includes them both. "His counterpart": the term includes two things, her existence, which without his is unthinkable, and vice versa. This is the promise that is made to man and woman in Jesus Christ, that in the painful sickness and corruption of their relationship they may know that this relationship of being a counterpart fulfills the relationship of Jesus Christ to his church (Eph. 5:22–33), and that from now on they may live as those who "from the very beginning" met each other thus. For from the beginning their relationship as counterparts was destined by the "great mystery" (Eph. 5:32).

Anyone who tries to understand the relationship between men and women without this "mystery" will naturally misunderstand the position of women. Anyone who does not know of the subordination that has taken place will inevitably understand the position of subordination as being limited, will be unable to grasp the honor and dignity of this responsibility that belongs to women. But Paul understood it. He knew a woman in her position corresponds to the position that each Christian, including himself the apostle, must take in reference to the Lord. To be sure, it is only a metaphor. But as such it bears a special promise and may therefore become a testimony (see 1 Pet. 3:1). The apostle will not fail to find this testimony in the gatherings of the church. The church needs it. It needs the reminder of its subordination. Therefore women are by no means put to one side, as less gifted members of the church, but will be "used" with special distinction as women. They will be called upon to perform the ministry that only they can perform, and thus to fulfill their destiny. Behind the silence urged on women we see not an inability to speak but the recognition of their task. They too are learners (1 Cor. 14:35), "students of the Word of God" (Calvin). In acknowledging this they can refrain from using the gifts of grace that have been given to them for the sake of the ministry that builds up the church. Thus in the contrast between the silence of the women and the speaking of the men we can see the limits of all human speech, and the listening church, *ecclesia audiens,* is seen as the counterpart of the *ecclesia docens,* the teaching church. Who would dare to say that one was less than the other?

III

The testimony and therefore the form of the obedience that women are to render will be different at different times and in different situations. Thus we are not only allowed to ask but must ask whether the testimony Paul called for in those days in Corinth is obligatory for us today in the same form: that is, whether still today women are required to keep silent in worship.

These words of Paul (and also 1 Tim. 2:12; compare my *Die wirkliche Frau,* pp. 52ff.) have been in every age and in almost all churches held up to women as a warning sign: the rule here is YOU MUST NOT SPEAK! There can be no doubt that such use of the word of God is unspiritual and therefore impermissible, whatever one's stand is on the specific issues.

It is troubling that the answer of women—including Christian women—is generally not to point out the illegitimacy of such use of scripture but to turn away from Paul in sorrow or anger at the misogyny that led him to make such regretable statements. For example, we can find in the foreword to Pearl Buck's book *The Exile,* the biography of her mother,

> For my father my mother was only a woman. Since those days when I saw her whole being overshadowed [her husband had forbidden her to share in his missionary work] I have been the wholehearted enemy of Saint Paul. And every woman must feel the same way because of what he has done in the past to women . . . proud free-born women who were still damned, only because they were women. For their sake I am happy that in these new days his power is at an end.

It is not Paul who has "done" something to women—and thank God that today we can still hear his testimony in this question—but his interpreters. In theological commentaries we can read amazing things about 1 Corinthians 13:14 and 14:34. See, for example, in the work of Delling, "Paulus Stellung zu Frau und Ehe," 1931 (*Beiträge zur Wissenschaft von Altem Testament und Neuem Testament, IV,* Heft 5, p. 106) his comments on 1 Corinthians 11:7:

> This means that God and the man have an area of activity from which they derive their power and majesty in relation to the inferiority of those whom they influence. Just as the man is the reflection of God's glory through which the power and majesty of God are visible both toward the Lord and toward the created realm, so also the woman is a reflection of the man, in which his authority can and should develop.

Let me mention here that as early as 1902 a theologian like Fritz Barth in a public address called on his hearers to listen to the testimony of the New Testament about women, and to bring finally into play the specific Christian concept of woman. The present widespread idea of women is at best Jewish, or even pagan. According to it women are totally dependent beings, good enough to satisfy a man's drives, to bring him a rich dowry, to cook well for him, to give him children and then take care of them. In society she is a polished exhibit that advertises her husband's good taste and the success of his business. . . . In a man's realm of ideas (if he has any) she is seldom welcome, and when she is, it is so that she can agree with him. . . . And then complain about how limited women are! . . . But men continue to hold that the place of women and stoves is in the house; they are born to serve; and Goethe was right when he said, 'Let women learn early to serve, according to their destiny.' Those are fine words, but many a woman has been destroyed by those views.

Barth demanded a radical rejection of the idea that a woman is only a second-grade man. He also demanded better education for young women for positions in the professions and revision of the laws wherever they were one-sided in favor of men. ("Die Frauenfrage und das Christentum," in *Christus und Hoffnung* [Bern, 1913], pp. 156–157.)

The apostolic exhortations and commands are not codes of law but living instructions, which point in a specific direction and delineate a specific area within which we must hear today the instruction given then. They still have something quite specific to say to us today.

Thus we are not trying to undermine the timeless value of the presupposition for Paul's exhortations: that women, within the order which determines the relationship between men and women, are in a subordinate position. In saying this we find ourselves in opposition to a tendency that is widespread in progressive feminist circles today, a tendency to attack this presupposition and, where possible, to eliminate it as a concept that may have corresponded to the position of women in those days but which is today outmoded and out of place. Today it is advisable not to speak any longer of a difference in the position and function of men and women, because today, aside from psychological and biological differences which are admitted, it is acceptable to speak only of equality in all areas. Inasfar as the speaker still has a Christian orientation, reference is made to Galatians 3:28 and praise given to the insight that was vouchsafed there to Paul, in contrast to his rather fatal utterances in the First Epistle to the Corinthians.

To do justice to these "progressive" positions it is necessary to see them against the background that even today many women have no concept of the problem, are far from taking any independent responsibility, and without thinking accept the way things are, chosing the easy path of a peaceful arrangement with their husband, especially if he is widely influential in social and economic circles. Christian women then usually like to speak of God's will that they be submissive and thus give to their unthinking complacency the appearance of a decision to be obedient.

Paul's exhortation to women lies between these two possibilities, the "progressive" and the "reactionary." In both cases the concept of *hypotage*, submission, is burdened by a preconception that does not correspond to the intention of the apostle. In both cases one "knows" a priori who is the husband, and who is the wife, and what the system is in which they are both placed. In each case there is a program involved, either aggressive or passive. Thus it is understandable that those on one side regard the exhortation to submission as an unreasonable demand and the others as the confirmation of their unreflective and largely bourgeois indolence. Paul is not interested in these alternatives, but in the obedience of Christians to the system in which God has placed man and woman, and especially in the obedience of women, because their position corresponds to that of the Christian community and also because this position is specifically useful in the community. It is here that the natural order first becomes evident in its own significance and in terms of its ultimate basis. Only where its fulfillment in Jesus Christ and his community is known can it be known that the creation of human beings in the duality of man and woman as a metaphor for this fulfillment is a grace-filled command. By confronting human beings with their fellow humans from the start, confronting them with fellow humans of the opposite sex, the man with the woman, the woman with the man, so that only together are they the human being that God desired and chose, God created them, not to be lonely, but in the way of life in which they encounter each other as an I and a Thou. In this way he prepared them for the encounter with the human Thou who is also the divine I. This encounter takes place in the community which the Lord indeed chose as his counterpart. The relationship of man and woman as counterparts can only be a metaphor for this other relation of counterparts which the Letter to the Ephesians terms "a great mystery" (5:32). As a metaphor however it can become a sign of the matter itself: man and woman can understand that each is the counterpart of the other, and, in the light of the event which was fulfilled in Jesus Christ, each of them can recognize the position and function granted to each as the promise and demand of the divine commandment.

It is here that their difference from each other in their unity becomes significant. Anyone who objects that we are not dealing here with identical but with differentiated partners that are not interchangeable at will, but have been placed in a specific system, will not have understood that it is precisely the differentiation that guarantees the independence of each and also their equality of birth as counterparts to each other. Here each one must assume his or her responsibility, for here each is addressed in the place and in the position that is decreed within the shared order by God's command. Here each must give his or her answer, which will so harmonize with that of the other that the unity of the human couple will be made known. If human existence as man and woman is understood as a given that they are to transcend, as a "situation," then for the woman the differentiation will become a burden that should not be taken too seriously. The all-decisive point here is that human sexual destiny be recognized as constitutive and definitive for human existence. But this can be recognized only where we know that it is a part of the uniqueness of human life as willed and bestowed by God that a person is either man or woman, that thus the promise and the claim of God's command always involves this destiny as well. It is the glory of man and woman that they, as such, as man and as woman, are addressed by God. Where this is recognized there is no room for any comparative evaluation.

Seen in this way, each can discover himself or herself only as a thankful creature of God in the place assigned by God. Won't the woman who knows this, free then of any inferiority complex in relation to a man, accept surely in joy and calmness (it is no accident that the concept of *hesychia*, "stillness," is found in the same context as *hypotage*, "submission"; see 1 Tim. 2:11–12; 1 Pet. 3:4) that she is a woman and not a man? Don't all these efforts to make the distinction between man and woman insignificant, or even to deny it altogether, conceal an uncertainty in women as to whether their position and function, in relation to that of men, might be lesser and therefore of less value? And doesn't this uncertainty spring from a widespread but false interpretation of the concept of subordination? Of course, to take a position of subordination *(hypotassesthai)* means to assume in a specific order the position of a partner to one in a higher position, to recognize this other person in his or her position, so that both fit together and watch over the other. Who will say then that the position of the woman, because it is subordinate, is a position of dependency or of lesser value? Certainly not Paul. He summons women to take up their responsibility and independence. Woman does not receive the direction from a man; it is not a man's wish or will that is the criterion for her decision to obey, but only God's command to her that she accept her position.

We should not at this point anticipate what concrete decisions women should take here and now, and nothing would be more fraught with danger than to work here with blueprints or roles, whether that of the *"femme libre"* or that of the "Marian woman," whether that of the rebel or that of the submissive "eternal feminine." It could be that women today are called upon—and there are many indications that this is true—to assume in greater independence than heretofore their responsibilities in public life, and not to leave this to a few other women. Nor would they where possible in practical matters (in voting, for example) distance themselves with the foolish and always slightly coquettish remark, "We like to leave that to our men." It could be that way, but not necessarily in everything. It might also be that in concrete cases the decision of women to be obedient would require caution and reserve. Neither of these is a priori preferable, and the concept of submission does not require it. The content of the decision is by no means predetermined, but women in their thinking, speaking, and acting will not reject the place that is indicated for them, that they perceive as their responsibility for the order in which they stand together with men.

This brings us back to the concrete question we are considering here. Is it demanded of women even today that they give up the idea of participating actively in the ministry of the proclamation of the word in the gatherings of the church? Does the church today still need the testimony of their silence, or does it need instead a different testimony?

We have heard of all the variety in the worship services of the church in Corinth—and more or less in early Christian worship in general: how the voices of the prophets, the muttering or speaking in tongues, the psalms and hymns, not to mention the ecstatic jubilation at the festival meals, all mingled with one another, so that the apostle could only with difficulty calm people down and restore order by reminding them of the edification of the community, which is the goal of worship and to which the church must devote itself. For it is not these things but the Lord himself who builds up his church through the ministry that is performed in love.

And today? Today the whole congregation keeps quiet, the men and the women, and only a few songs—and, in more liturgical churches, perhaps even responsorial psalms—before and after the sermon break into this silence of the congregation. One man speaks, Sunday after Sunday, some times also on weekday evenings, and proclaims God's word to the congregation. This man has studied theology, he has passed his examinations, he has served as a vicar and shown that he is competent, and now he has been called and installed by the congregation to this ministry. He leads worship in the gatherings for worship in loneliness over against the congregation, who, at least outwardly, are almost totally passive. The fullness of voices is silenced, the work of the Holy Spirit—at most—is done by one voice. "If a pastor does not display a life of faith, or if a preacher proclaims only one special message, and that in a one-sided manner, this gives a particular stamp to the whole congregation. . . . In the early church it was different . . . in our miserable one-man system we are compelled to shape the whole congregation by our one-sidedness." (Eduard Schweizer, "Die Urchristenheit als ökumenische Gemeinschaft," in *Evangelische Theologie,* 1950/51, p. 287.)

Among all these silent people, can silence still be a testimony? Does the church today need to have its enthusiastic excesses dampened, or does it not much more need a reminder that all members are called to ministry in the church? To be sure, we cannot force the Holy Spirit and the Spirit's gift to be present, but we can and must plead for the coming of the Spirit and, if possible, not confine the breadth of the Spirit through our unbelief within too narrow limits. (See F. J. Leenhardt, "Die Stellung der Frau im Neuen Testament," in *Kirchliche Zeitfragen,* 24 [Zurich, 1949], p. 55.) In addition, such a narrow limit threatens the understanding of "office" that has developed in the Protestant churches.

In view of this situation, the question arises whether the testimony of women in the churches today, in contrast to their silence in the church of Corinth, should not be through speaking: that is, should it be possible to call women to the ministry of proclaiming the word? There is little doubt but that, because of the church of pastors and theologians we have today, there will be a call for a new consideration of the New Testament understanding of church offices as ministry in the congregation. Isn't it possible for women to make a contribution that men cannot make in the same manner? They will be able to make this contribution only if in obedience to their position as women they receive a definite call to this ministry. They will thus by no means push themselves into this ministry on the grounds of "equal rights" or "equal position" with men, as is now happening is so many other areas, including the church. Nor should it be on the basis that the "contribution of women" should not be lacking in this area either, in as far as the psychological contribution is concerned. Women need to be called to this ministry if they are to share in this work legitimately. This call will be apparent in that their sharing in the building up of the congregation is as much needed today as their silence was once. It should be clear that the witness of women today should not reinforce the passivity of the congregation. The church today needs to be awakened to active participation, and therefore the witness of women could consist in coming forward and committing themselves to the word, in their being called to active ministry of the word.

In emergency situations, such as war, when men are prevented from carrying out the duties of their offices, it happens that women are called to this ministry. But emergencies create emergency measures and cannot provide basic authorization. Thus, with a few exceptions, it was only after the war that people began to explore the question of whether women should be "admitted" to this ministry, without any clear conclusions being reached thus far. In reality there are women in this ministry in almost all countries, but still burdened with uncertainty as to whether they are doing so legitimately. If it were a matter of calling women "officers" in addition to the men, the response would probably be in the negative, especially in churches where the supply exceeds the demand. But the issue is not whether to supplement the number of pastors through adding a few women, but whether women as ministers of the word can make an essential contribution to the necessary transformation of this "office." By their natural position, women are less likely to claim authority and thus as ministers of the divine word are less tempted to an authoritarian view of their ministry. This means they would be less tempted than men are to obscure the authority of the word through the authority of their person. We have heard that their natural position corresponds to that of the church, and so they are advised to perform their ministry in obedience, even as servants of the word, standing not above but in the midst of their congregation. They will work, therefore, not at a distance but in their person to bring the office and the congregation together, without detracting in the least from the authority of the ministry that has been entrusted to them. It is then that the authority of the word, and not of the person, will be evident.

"It would be instructive," says Franz Josef Leenhardt (pp. 53–54), "to investigate to what extent Christian preaching, theology, and the souls that have been entrusted to us, have suffered because of the exclusive preponderance of the male nature. Nothing indicates that the pastoral office as it has been administered under male influence is the only possible or desirable form of that office." With this quotation we do not want to enter the area of psychological findings, but only to call attention to the importance of the differing position and function of men and women for this ministry.

Women still have ahead of them, considering the whole picture, the final shaping of their ministry in the proclamation of the word. This may then be their chance, if they recognize their special task: if, that is, they are not content to be only successful imitations of the "Reverend Pastor" but seek their own place. They will then find their ministry as simple members of the community, remembering that each is called to minister with the gift entrusted to him or her by God. They will respect the gifts of the other members of the congregation and let them come into action, and also subordinate their gifts, if that is called for. They will not anxiously seek to monopolize the proclamation, but on the other hand they will undertake on their own initiative ministries such as those performed by the widows in the New Testament, which were encouraged as "good works" (1 Tim. 5:10), works of compassion. The "striking prominence of the preacher has misled us to see the entire life of the church of Jesus as consisting in talking. Thus the teaching that was so important, even central in the New Testament, had been cast in the form of a monopoly, so that we have fully forgotten that there can be members of the congregation who have less formal education than we do, but who nevertheless have a faith that is stronger and more productive than ours" (Schweizer). They will certainly not neglect their central task, but they will show it is not carried out in isolation, yet can only be performed in the community, and that the gift is useless unless it is given in love. They will—and this is not a matter of indifference—probably find their own style in the externals (perhaps even giving up the robes of office!), and so also give expression to the insight that it is not the "office" that is important but the ministry that is intrusted to them.

These suggestions are not meant to lead to a program but are searchlights to show the direction in which women in the formation of their ministry can show solidarity with the congregation and can help to overcome the division that has developed between the church officials and the congregation. The concrete decisions, as is self-evident, will have to be made at the appropriate times and in the appropriate places.

Women confront a difficult task when they are called to the ministry of the word, a task that is impossibly difficult if they cannot bring their position as women into harmony with that ministry. They are confronted with the "office of pastor" as defined by men and must come to terms with it. Either they will simply conform to it or they will transform it on the basis of a newly acquired understanding of "ministry." If they find their own way and recognize the commission entrusted to them, if they carry out in obedience the proper proclamation and in the proper way lead the congregation through God's word, then in joyful certainty they will carry on their ministry so that they will bear that testimony which is required of them and which is essential to the upbuilding of the church.

The practical decision of the outward calling of women to the ministry of proclaiming the word will have to be made by the congregation itself. But this does not mean that women will have to wait passively for the leaders of the church to make their decision. They also are members of the church, and thus they also are called to share the responsibility and the work that comes with it. Thus they are by no means only objects of the call but, throughout the process, are helping to made the decision.

In conclusion I would like to quote an Anglican theologian, R. W. Howard. He delivered three lectures on our theme at Oxford University. At first a passionate opponent, he came, as the result of thorough study of the entire scope of the problem, to an unqualified affirmation of the admission of women to the pastoral office. The lectures appeared under the title *Should Women Be Priests?* (Oxford: Basil Blackwell, 1949).

Howard concludes by commenting that those women who are involved in the pioneering work for the full office of priest

> must have the deep humility and love which will enable them to undertake lowly service that will often seem unworthy of their powers. They must cultivate an unquenchable sense of humour that will help them to smile at the outmoded prejudice of the men and women who will deride or hinder their work. Above all, they will need the spirit of true devotion to our Lord Jesus Christ, and to those to

whom He wills to send them. . . . It may be—surely it must be—that if enough such women can be found to act as pioneers, our Church as a whole will one day come to recognize this devotion and service as a genuine answer to a genuine call from God: a call so clear and unmistakable that first the Church, and then the bishops, will not dare any longer to refuse to identify the call as being the clear command of the Holy Spirit.

Epilogue
by Hans Prolingheuer

"We may wonder whether Karl Barth was not influenced much more than he realized by the peculiar circumstances of his private life, rather than being basically influenced by the Holy Scriptures. Not a few persons would regard this as a painful tragedy." This malicious statement is found in the pastoral letter issued by Hanover Regional Bishop August Marahrens on July 17, 1935. It was part of the final revenge of the victor in the struggle for the leadership of the Confessing Church.

After weeks of political and theological battles, the Confessing Church had finally decided for Marahrens, the intimate friend of Minister of the Interior Hans Frick, and against the socialist "traitor" Karl Barth, and then had driven this political foreign body out of its ranks and thus out of Germany.

The German Protestant Church of the Third Reich had already accepted Bishop Marahrens' verdict that it was a threat to the offices of the church and damaging to the profession that "Karl Barth was not so committed to the new political reality in Germany as I feel it was obvious he should be." Thus the malicious allusion to Barth's private life had only one purpose: in addition to the political and professional condemnation of the antifascist Karl Barth, now to add moral condemnation.

16. Caricature of the German church leaders who opposed Barth's political stance.

When forty years later, in my research into the "Case of Karl Barth" during the years 1934–35, I discovered the pastoral letter of Barth's enemy and read this infamous statement, I knew at once what Marahrens was alluding to. I had known since 1967, when I served as the director of the German Protestant Church Day in Hanover. No lesser a person than Marahrens' successor, the Hanover Bishop Hans Lilje, had confided in me.

In my office in the Leibnizufer, Leni Schutt (1901–1981), was working. During the Nazi era she had been business manager of the Confessing Community in Hanover and was known for her committed work against the regional leadership of the "German Christians." Her friendship with Bishop and Mrs. Lilje and her knowledge of persons and places in the region were a great help to me. She came out of retirement and was able to help the bishop as a supplementary source of information about the status of preparations for the Church Day.

Whenever Bishop Lilje visited my fellow worker with a bottle of wine, he bragged about her having been one of the first recipients of the Distinguished Service Award of the Federal Republic. "She was the only *man* in the Confessing Church," he said. Every time he praised her in this way she grew irritated and called down strong imprecations on this "male-dominated church." Then she would call out to her friend a whole list of forgotten "women of the church." And in answer to this provocation the bishop would call back more women's names—including, on one occasion, "Charlotte von Kirschbaum."

I inquired about the sudden heated nature of the exchange. And both of them then took great pains to initiate into the secret the poor innocent that I was. "But please, in confidence."

And in this conversation in the spring of 1967 I heard the same conclusions Marahrens had drawn in his pastoral letter. Both spoke of "too great expectations." And Bishop Lilje, who had studied under Barth in Göttingen, saw the reasons why Barth could not continue to reside in Germany not in Barth's theology but in his private life. I objected that Barth's private life was probably only used by his theological and political opponents in order to avoid the uncomfortable demands of his theology, but Lilje stoutly denied this.

What I only surmised in 1967 I later found confirmed by the pastoral letter of Barth's opponent, Marahrens. And since then I have become aware of all the other "gossips" of whom Rose Marie Barth speaks in her prologue to this book. I think, first, of all those petty figures in the church and in theology for whom "Karl and Lollo" is an inexhaustible topic of conversation hour after hour in the house bars at meetings of Protestant bodies, and then of those who are always ready when there is an opportunity to cast the first stone.

I think also of those always-calm "Barthians" who, like epigones, spread their little theological discoveries and biographical anecdotes among the people of the church, but who avoid the name of Charlotte von Kirschbaum like the plague and, acting like governesses his part of Barth's biography; while in their quiet little studies they ask, in a hurt and secretive manner, how Karl Barth could possibly have brought this shame on them.

And I remember all too well how both types—the gossipy little people and the aforesaid "Barthians"— chattered and gossiped when, in 1977, two years after Charlotte von Kirschbaum's death, in the introduction to my book *Der Fall Karl Barth 1934– 1935, Chronographie einer Vertreibung* ("The Case of Karl Barth, 1934–1935, Chronology of a Banishment"), I mentioned at one point in the introduction, "There in Karl Barth's tomb in the Hörnli Cemetery in Riehen on the right bank of the Rhine, Karl Barth's faithful co-worker Charlotte von Kirschbaum found her final resting place in 1975." The four words "in Karl Barth's tomb" provided the gossips with more nourishment than all 432 book pages together, pages in which the ecclesiastical and political scandal of Karl Barth's banishment from the Confessing Church is documented.

Since then I have hoped and urged that those who are respectable would put an end to this unworthy game. Karl Barth and Charlotte von Kirschbaum never concealed from anyone or played down their extremely vulnerable relationship. Why should we leave this part of the biography to the attacks of those whose political activity is carried on at the keyhole? Veneration of a theological hero is precisely the opposite of what Barth taught and preached.

But there is also another reason for sticking to the biographical truth. In not doing so, a woman is offered as a sacrifice to the icon of "Karl the Great of Protestant Theology," a woman without whom the "probably most significant theologian since Luther and Calvin" would not have existed. And there on the antifeminine side of prettying up the church and theology was the starting point for this work.

In the summer semester of 1984 Renate Köbler, then in the eighth semester of her theological studies, asked me during my major seminar at Marburg in church history to suggest a theme for the seminar paper. Since she made it clear that she did not want merely to review what was already written but to do original research, and since she was particularly interested in women in the recent history of the Protestant church, I introduced her to Karl Barth's co-worker, who had been consigned to forgetfulness, making clear to her from the start the unusual difficulty of such an undertaking.

When the Barth family agreed and friends of Karl Barth and Charlotte von Kirschbaum expressed their willingness to help, the twenty-four-year-old student fell to work. Toward the end of the winter semester, after much travel, many conversations, and extensive correspondence, she placed before me a result that was more than just an outstanding seminar paper. While she was still carrying out her research, I suggested to her, with the support of Helmut Gollwitzer, that she plan to publish what would be the first account of Charlotte von Kirschbaum's life but, in any case, to write an article about her for the journal *Junge Kirche*, called "Eine Zeitschrift europaischer Christen," as a memorial on the tenth anniversary of her death. And this impressively sketched first portrait—seven pages in the July 1985 issue of this journal (which, together with the old *Stimmen der Zeit,* was highly valued by both Karl Barth and Charlotte von Kirschbaum), had an impact beyond the circle of the journal's readers.

Because the editors had unfortunately eliminated the introduction which was to accompany the article, and which told of the origin of the article and the cooperation of Barth's family and friends and gave information about the author, some readers had a feeling of betrayal. In their search for the persons behind the article they wanted to know "where Renate Köbler got her intimate information." The majority of those who read the article, however, reacted favorably, and an unusually large number of letters were received. Here is a selection from the numerous queries, suggestions, expressions of thanks, and personal memories sent to the author.

Klaus-Dieter Stoll, Heidelberg: "Everyone should insert the article in Eberhard Busch's *Karl Barth.* I hope that the theme of Charlotte von Kirschbaum will be developed further, especially since I believe that she could be the ideal point of contact and stimulation for feminist theology today."

Dr. Anna Sticker, Düsseldorf-Kaiserswerth: "Since 1923 I have been serving as deaconess in Kaiserswerth. After my studies and two years as a teacher in a secondary school, I was placed in charge of the Library for the Diaconate of Women and the Fliedner Archives. There I prepared the *Kaiserswerther Mitteilungen* and the *Brazilnachrichten* and other periodicals, which were then signed by my supervisors. The longer this went on the harder it was for me to bear that in an institute for women, work done by women was published under the names of men. For all my work as a deaconess I received, as did von Kirschbaum, only pocket money. . . . Then there came a breakthrough with my two books about Friederike Fliedner and the development of modern nursing. For these works I received on my seventieth birthday an honorary doctorate from the Theological Faculty in Bonn. . . . Why do I feel I must tell you this? Posthumous recognition for Charlotte von Kirschbaum—that is the case for many women theologians today who must lead their life in the shadows. I regard it as my task in life to help the nursing profession escape from life in the shadows."

Werner Koch, Emlichheim: "I regard it as a great contribution that you have gone to the trouble of reviving in so understanding a way the memory of 'Lollo' on the occasion of the tenth anniversary of her death. May I ask if you knew her personally? . . . In December 1932 Barth invited me for the first time to share a meal with him. Afterward Barth, Lollo, and I went upstairs to the study. Lollo prepared tea, as she always did. This scene was often repeated over the decades."

Elizabeth and Martin Giesen, Cologne: "Have you ever reflected, dear candidate in theology, how Mrs. Nelly Barth contributed her life and her powers for the success of Karl Barth's work? My wife responded in a practical manner: Who peeled the potatoes, cooked the meals, served the many guests, washed the laundry? [Mrs. Barth naturally had qualified personnel to take care of the housework and to care for the children—H.P.] Don't you feel challenged to write a further work—about Nelly Barth? Is she not a heroine of faithfulness and a readiness to forgive again and again? It is not only professional women who deserve public mention. In our opinion many marriage partners and mothers in their shadow existence perform at least as much significant service as do the comparable professional women."

Marguerite Thurneysen, Basel: "I was very close to Charlotte von Kirschbaum, and I recognize her clearly in your portrayal. How much time you must have spent in your preparation for this article! Now at last Lollo's contribution, her unlimited commitment, her theological work is appreciated, and she does not sink entirely into the 'shadows.' My husband [Eduard Thurneysen, surely Karl Barth's most trusted friend—H.P.] and I shared closely the enigmatic life of Karl Barth, his wife, and Lollo—and affirmed that life. Too many knew only how to criticize."

Eberhard Busch, Uerkheim: "I am not at all satisfied with the title you chose for your work, and which reflects your bias. But I will not involve myself at all in that question, for that is your responsibility. But you yourself must surely know that in this way you have placed 'Lollo' in a shadow in which she, I am certain, did not see her life. Lollo to be sure stood in a shadow, and after her death she truly entered the shadows. But in my opinion this is decisively connected with the fact that she with unheard-of bravery entered into a very unconventional life—as an unmarried woman 'at the side' of a married theologian, as a result of which her life was lived constantly in a position which was regarded with contempt by society (and by many 'Barthians' with disgust)."

Karl Handrich, Landau: "Karl Barth and his dear wife Nelly and Lollo (as well as his sons) were often our guests, and we were theirs in Basel. My wife and I knew the problematic nature of this unique community and were always astonished how splendidly they managed it, even with all the difficulties. A famous professor of theology in Germany once described Lollo von Kirschbaum as a 'theological bluestocking.' "

Uvo A. Wolf, Sonnenbühl: "I am grateful for having had through my father [Professor Ernst Wolf], and also during my own years of study in Basel in 1959–61, frequent contact with these two persons, and on occasion also with Mrs. Nelly Barth. The tensions could be felt, and still it is necessary to speak, more clearly than Gollwitzer did, of 'providence.' In any case, it is more important for me to ask whether Lollo's contribution to the 'equality of opportunity for women' has not been made outdated by the so-called 'feminist' theology. If we bring this beginning together with the 'primacy of ministry' on the part of the men—and this by analogy to the sacrificing-oneself-for-the-congregation—then it will hardly be possible to find an approach with better theological foundations. But these comments are only marginal notes. My sincerest thanks for your good and important contribution."

Johannes Merz, Augsburg: "To identify myself, let me say that I am the youngest son of the frequently quoted Georg Merz. Thus I have read this article with interest, especially because it brings back memories of my youth. For us 'Aunt Lollo' was a beloved family aunt, godmother to my sister, who is at present director of a home for the aged, and who continued to correspond with 'Aunt Lollo' until the onset of her illness. From that point of view you will perhaps (even with laughter) understand that we take the 'all too personal' quite differently. . . . Hers was definitely not a 'shadow existence.' The background was very quickly discovered by many students who lived in our house, and passionately discussed to the point of despair. And in reference to your final sentence about pocket money, 'Lollo' lives in my memory as a lady, with all that belongs to that term—her charm, the clothes she wore, her self-confident bearing, and also the many valuable gifts that she regularly gave to her godchildren. . . . I would rather imagine that in addition to her position she worked as 'well-paid' reader for a publishing firm, as was customary at that time for other authors as well. . . . Apart from that, my father was never a 'nationalist, conservative.' . . . Agreed that to the derision of Karl Barth, my father, having been deprived of his office by the Nazis, returned to his Bavarian church home—indeed, a regional church of conservative character—and became Dean in Würzburg. But until his death he remained one of the most independent-minded personalities of that church."

Markus Wildi, Aarau: "You may know that in 1980 for my diploma in library science I wrote about Barth's writings that had been published separately, and in historical retrospect I also wanted to include Lollo, but I had a damned lot of trouble to find anything published about her. In our library I could not even find her father's first name.... I was very fond of Lollo and as a student had known her personally and had conversed with her on several occasions. I can vouch for the portrait of her that you sketched in your article as totally correct. I would like very much to have an opportunity to talk with you. I am now performing at least a part of the work that Lollo did for Barth throughout her life: compiling his bibliography. [In 1984 the first volume of the *Karl Barth Bibliography* was published, compiled by Wildi for the Karl Barth Foundation—H.P.] Thus I feel that in a sense I am her 'successor.'"

Franziska Zellweger, Basel/Gstaad: "It was very good of you to send me a copy of your *good* article on the life and work of L. von Kirschbaum. My brothers [Barth's two sons Christoph and Markus—H.P.] also read it with approval. . . . It is good that this life, which brought about so much that was positive, and yet also tragic, was presented in a worthy manner, and we hope that this will put a stop to some of the gossip."

When the ecumenical weekly *Neue Stimme* was beginning to publish the book manuscript in serial form (March to July 1986), Renate Köbler received a long letter from Nicaragua. The French theologian Georges Casalis, friend, comrade-in-arms, and biographer of Karl Barth, felt deeply moved by her article. As Eduard Thurneysen's son-in-law, he, with his wife, Dorothee, had planned to write about Charlotte von Kirschbaum's life soon after her death. The persistent silence of her contemporaries, however, made that task impossible. Thus their pleasure was all the greater when they received the unexpected article. His letter from Managua is thus more than an expression of thanks to the young author.

Dear Renate Köbler,
 You will be surprised to receive a letter from me, especially a letter from Nicaragua. This demonstrates that I was very moved by your article about Charlotte von Kirschbaum, and also that when I am on a long journey I take along unanswered mail in the hope of being able to take care of it between lectures and meetings. That is the case today: a couple of quiet hours before our transportation leaves for Somotillo on the Honduran border, and following four days in a seminar on "The Kingdom of God and Reconciliation" with fifty Protestant students of theology. . . . This made me think how Carolus and Lollo might have come here from Basel to take part. When I recall his excellent stand against the Vietnam war—see his letter to the Evangelicals who were assembled in Dortmund in 1966—I have no doubt but that he would regard the theologians of liberation and the groups in solidarity with the oppressed peoples of the Third World as his true successors, more so than those who today try to construct an orthodoxy, or a scholasticism, out of his theology. Be that as it may, I know too well how much I owe to him— and how he would laugh good-humoredly at himself—to ever be concerned about the genuineness of the adjective "Barthian" when applied to this or that group, or to me.
 Your article moved me very much for a number of reasons, which I would like to share with you.
 First, you fill a great lack, which we, together with Dorothee Thurneysen, immediately felt after Lollo's death as a great injustice. We had made plans to publish a book of tributes to her and had even sent out a circular letter. But to our surprise none of those we contacted really wanted to work with us. We encountered embarrassed silence, unanticipated reservations. People were

ready to love her and honor her secretly but not openly. Thus even those of us who considered ourselves progressive felt the weight of middle-class morality and the power of tabus, which immediately after Karl Barth's death descended over that side of his life. Voltaire himself wrote that you had better wait to canonize a person until none of his contemporaries are still alive. In this case it is the whole of Christianity that is ashamed of this woman and is ready, "because of her," to be ashamed of him and to regard him as still somewhat acceptable only when total silence is maintained about her. That is not the way he was. This is shown not only by the grave in Hörnli cemetery but also by many letters in which he acknowledged her in writing, and especially by the fact that in the fifties he declined to take part in the five hundredth anniversary of the University of Basel, not only as a speaker but in any capacity, because she had not been invited. I still remember how after the celebration he invited us and Heinrich Vogel to his house to hear him chuckle about how Karl Jaspers had spoken "in his stead"!

In short, we are happy and thankful for your article, and we hope that your book will be published soon. It must and will be the indispensable pendant to the larger and smaller biographies of the master.

Second, the worthy public wants to eradicate the triangle in the Barth house from history, as Stalin did to Trotsky and Krushchev did to Stalin, and not only because it is clear to Catholics (Josef Ratzinger!), and practical for Protestants, to regard sex as the essence of sin. ... As if in this case that was the primary issue! You have shown in exemplary fashion that it was a fully human congeniality in all areas of both their lives that led to this distinctive and extraordinary union. And in an amazing way the upright observers of this wonderful and tragic encounter are offended that no divorce took place, which they all would have forgotten after six months—or six years—and which today could be interpreted as an understandable incident in the life of a great man. There are none, even among us who were the closest friends of the three, who doubt that this impossible possibility, this never solved solution, was much more evangelical than any legal or geographical separation between Karl and Nelly could have been. As witnesses of this unusual life, it gradually became clear to us that in all the disruption and conflict among them there were also moments of relaxation, of mutual friendship, and above all that each of the three remained true to self and to the two others, and that all this was, in an exemplary way, suffered, but also truly experienced in all clarity and wisdom. And that at the end of Karl's life Nelly had again become the one closest to him was then and is now deeply moving to us. Please understand that we do not desire either to justify or to understand everything, but to refrain from any legalistic judgment and to believe that this example, which neither should nor could become in any way a model, was not outside the grace of God nor unfruitful. . . .

Third, we belong to the earlier generation of students and friends who during the Second World War experienced all these events in Basel and at Bergli. During the war we were often together with Karl and Lollo. Later they were from time to time our guests in Strassburg, and finally in Paris, when her illness had become far advanced. We often witnessed their radiant happiness. . . . Dorothee was bound to them by ties of friendship and wonder; I, like almost all students in those days, was in love with her. I am surprised that you portray her as more "Barthian than Barth," abrupt and intolerant. Quite the contrary. We were often very grateful that with gentleness and a smile, with "womanly" intuition and finesse, she knew how to put things right and thus to mediate matters that people would not so easily have taken directly from him. In addition, she was from time to time a very welcome, patient tutor, through whom it was granted to us to penetrate into the final depths of the *Church Dogmatics*. . . . Perhaps this was, as we French like to say, "the iron fist in a velvet glove," but it helped us, and I myself can confess that in this way her often very sharp criticism brought me farther than the occasional verdict delivered by him "vertically from above," though others may have experienced it differently.

But under this last point I am concerned with the real question which I have in relation to your article. From the lines I wrote immediately after her death in August 1975 (which appeared in the journal *Réforme*) you can see that for us, and especially for me, she was the one who opened the door to the feminist reading of scripture, to the creative entry of women into theology, and to a new understanding of the relationship between men and women in politics, in the church, and in love. . . . This was and will remain her historical role, and that this was not only possible but even necessary, in her shared life with Karl, is a very important sign of the healthiness of his theological existence.

You, and we, write forty years after the publication of *Die wirkliche Frau*. In the intervening years we men, thanks to the demands of feminist theology and its authors, have made some progress, although the way to full realization of the equality of the "two halves of heaven" still seems very narrow and steep. . . . And I sense through what you have written the demanding tone and somewhat aggressive spirit that is inseparable from the struggle of women for liberation. You have a degree of sympathy with Lollo, because she was "exploited" economically and as a human being and thus did not come to her full development, to her full rights as a woman. . . . How do you know that? This very beautiful woman was always dressed simply but elegantly, with jewelry and lovely hats. From time to time she gave expensive gifts that must have cost somewhat more than the "pocket money" you assume was her lot. She would probably have laughed ironically if anyone had told her that she was a victim of machismo, and not only because these were questions not generally recognized in her day and in her Christian environment, quite different from Marxist and humanist circles to be sure. For her he was the meaning and center of her existence. She was totally caught up in her love for him, and in this total commitment to him expended herself and burnt herself out. She disappeared into intellectual night in the moment he ceased to write. . . .

You know that we, like you, are totally engaged in the struggles for justice and liberation to the end. But along the way there is still, and always will be, the miracle of love, which demands for itself only to be permitted to love and be loved. That is the ultimate mystery of the invaluable and in many respects exemplary existence of this real woman, Charlotte von Kirschbaum. . . . The individual should never let us forget the duty to be committed to justice to the very end. But the struggle for justice must also respect and accept individuals in their surprising and many-sided forms. Otherwise we know only too well where that road leads. . . .

We thank you again for rescuing Charlotte von Kirschbaum from the pharisaical fate of being thankfully forgotten, and hope that you agree with our plan to have this letter published in the *Junge Kirche*. [It appeared there in May 1986, pp 290–292—H.P.]

In heartfelt unity,
(Signed) Georges Casalis

Notes

Introduction

1. "Work in the shadows" is a phrase coined by Ivan Illich. By it he means "the modern, unremunerated counterpart of work for wages.... Work in the shadows is not only work at a subsistence level.... It does not provide for the household, but produces finished goods without pay." Illich uses the term not only in reference to housework, even though that is the prototype of work in the shadows, but also in reference to all unpaid work in society (Illich, *Vom Recht auf Gemeinheit* [Hamburg, 1982], pp. 75–93). I have taken this term and applied it also to scholarly work.

2. Karl Barth, *Church Dogmatics* (hereafter *CD* [ET, Edinburgh, T.&T. Clark, 1960]), III/3, Preface, pp. xii–xiii.

3. These two biographies of Barth are Eberhard Busch, *Karl Barths Lebenslauf* (Munich, 3rd ed., 1978; ET *Karl Barth, His Life from Letters and Autobiographical Texts* [Philadelphia: Fortress Press, 1976]); and Karl Küpisch, *Karl Barth in Selbstzeugnissen und Bilddokumenten* (Stuttgart, 1977).

4. Gerhard Wehr, *Karl Barth—Theologe und Gottes fröhlicher partisan* (Gütersloh, 1979).

5. Corr. G. Casalis. (Here and throughout, see Unpublished Sources in Bibliography for conversations, correspondence, and unpublished documents.)

Chapter 1: Childhood and Youth

1. Conv. W. v. Kirschbaum.
2. Unpub. doc. Barth family.

3. The words "stilted atmosphere of an officer's household" were used by Helmut Gollwitzer in our conversation to describe the Kirschbaum home.
4. Unpub. doc. Barth family.
5. Ibid.
6. Conv. W. v. Kirschbaum.
7. The places and dates mentioned in these two paragraphs were also supplied by Wolf von Kirschbaum in our conversation.
8. Unpub. doc. Barth family.
9. Unpub. doc. W. v. Kirschbaum.
10. Conv. W. v. Kirschbaum.
11. Unpub. doc. Barth family.
12. This information and the quotation were taken from Corr. W. v. Kirschbaum. According to Dr. Lili Simon, a friend of Charlotte von Kirschbaum, Charlotte did *not* want to become a deaconess but, as was then appropriate for members of the nobility, a sister of the Order of St. John. Corr. E. Busch, August 3, 1985.
13. Corr. W. v. Kirschbaum. I can give only a limited impression of Charlotte von Kirschbaum's childhood and youth, since all those with whom I spoke about her learned to know her only when she was an adult, and she herself, as mentioned, spoke hardly at all of those years. Thus this chapter raises more questions than it can answer.

Chapter 2: Georg Merz, a Good Friend in the Early Years

1. Corr. W. v. Kirschbaum.
2. Eberhard Busch, *Karl Barth,* p. 125.
3. Conv. E. Busch.
4. Tel. conv. W. v. Kirschbaum, November 29, 1984.
5. Busch, *Barth,* p. 125.
6. See Karl Küpisch, *Karl Barth in Selbstzeugnissen und Bilddokumenten,* p. 41.
7. Busch, *Barth,* p. 131.
8. Ibid., pp. 158–159.
9. Ibid., p. 263, from a letter of Karl Barth to his son Christoph, December 29, 1959.
10. Ibid., p. 444.
11. Corr. W. v. Kirschbaum.
12. The assumption of an initial brief meeting between Charlotte von Kirschbaum and Karl Barth at a lecture Barth deliv-

Notes 143

ered in 1924, and the subsequent invitation to Switzerland, was mentioned by Busch in our conversation. He recalled this event from a personal conversation with Barth.

13. See Erica Küppers, "Auf dem Bergli," in *Stimme der Gemeinde* (1966), column 301. I have been unable to obtain any further information about Charlotte von Kirschbaum's first visit to Bergli, so what follows is a detailed report on her *second* journey to Switzerland, in 1925. The summer of 1925 remained a vivid memory, not only for those whom I consulted but also for Karl Barth. In the mid-thirties he recorded in a large book for the first time important autobiographical dates, including, for the summer of 1925, *Bergli, Lollo!* Corr. H. Stoevesandt.

Chapter 3: Bergli, a Place of Encounter

1. See Thurneysen to Barth, July 25, 1925, in Eduard Thurneysen, ed., *Karl Barth–Eduard Thurneysen, Briefwechsel 1921–1930*, p. 358.
2. Unpub. doc. Barth family.
3. Eberhard Busch, *Karl Barth,* p. 158.
4. Tel. conv. W. v. Kirschbaum, November 29, 1984.
5. Thurneysen to Barth August 31, 1925, in Thurneysen, *Briefwechsel,* pp. 366–367.
6. Corr. W. v. Kirschbaum.
7. Busch, *Barth,* p. 198.

Chapter 4: Stations on the Way to Shared Theological Work

1. Corr. W. v. Kirschbaum.
2. Unpub. doc. Barth family.
3. Quoted from corr. W. v. Kirschbaum.
4. See Eberhard Busch, *Karl Barth,* p. 178.
5. Corr. E. Busch, July 17, 1985.
6. Barth to Thurneysen, November 8, 1926, in Eduard Thurneysen, ed., *Briefwechsel,* p. 441.
7. Ibid., pp. 441–442.
8. Barth to Thurneysen, November 29, 1926, ibid., p. 448.
9. Barth to Thurneysen, April 13, 1927, ibid., p. 484.
10. Barth to Thurneysen, Dec. 26, 1926, ibid., p. 450.
11. Busch, *Barth,* p. 187.
12. Barth to Thurneysen, August 21, 1927, ibid., p. 515.

13. Barth to Thurneysen, September 17, 1927, ibid., p. 523.
14. Busch, *Barth*, p. 198.
15. Thus far I have been unable to establish definitely that Charlotte von Kirschbaum and Gertrud Staewen became acquainted during this time. Almost everyone with whom I talked independently expressed this surmise. But Rose Marie Barth is of the opinion that the two women had come to know each other earlier at Bergli.
16. Michael Popke (publisher for the Conference of Evangelical Church Partners in the Institute for Achieving Justice, West Berlin) *Schreien nach Gerechtigkeit* (In Honor of Gertrud Staewen on Her Ninetieth Birthday) (Berlin, 1984), pp. 56–57.
17. Ibid.
18. Unpub. doc. G. Staewen.

Chapter 5: Bergli, a Place of Shared Work

1. Eberhard Busch, *Karl Barth*, p. 198.
2. Corr. M. Barth.
3. Barth to Thurneysen, May 30, 1929, p. 662, in Thurneysen, *Brietwechsel*.
4. Barth to Thurneysen, July 3, 1929, ibid., p. 668.
5. Barth to Thurneysen, April 29, 1929, ibid., p. 660.
6. Unpub. doc. G. Staewen.
7. Conv. E. Busch.
8. Unpub. doc. G. Staewen.
9. Conv. E. Busch.
10. Conv. H. Gollwitzer.
11. On this point too all those I consulted were agreed that it was in the college for women in Berlin that she first came in contact with the women's movement. Unfortunately, it was not possible for me to meet with Gertrud Staewen, who would certainly have been able to supply more exact information. Note that while the term "women's emancipation" was used earlier, today in the women's movement "women's liberation" is more widely used.
12. Conv. H. Gollwitzer.

Chapter 6: Time Together, Work Together

1. Barth to Thurneysen, October 6, 1929, p. 679, in Thurneysen, *Briefwechsel*.

2. Conv. H. Gollwitzer.
3. Ibid.
4. Conv. R. M. Barth.
5. Eberhard Busch, *Karl Barth*, p. 199.
6. Conv. H. Gollwitzer.
7. Busch, *Barth*, p. 199.
8. Conv. W. v. Kirschbaum.
9. Tel. conv. W. v. Kirschbaum, March 15, 1985.
10. Busch, *Barth*, p. 199.
11. Conv. H. Gollwitzer.
12. Busch, *Barth*, p. 199.
13. Ibid.
14. Ibid.
15. Ibid.
16. Ibid.
17. Conv. M. Barth.
18. Busch, *Barth*, p. 199.
19. Statement by Dr. Lili Simon from corr. E. Busch, August 3, 1985.

Chapter 7: A Suitable Counterpart and Helper

1. Conv. H. Gollwitzer.
2. Barth to Thurneysen November 16, 1929, p. 686, in Thurneysen, *Briefwechsel*.
3. Barth to Thurneysen, November 16, 1929, ibid., pp. 688–689.
4. Barth to Thurneysen, January 26, 1930, ibid., p. 702.
5. Conv. E. Busch and conv. H. Gollwitzer.
6. Conv. H. Gollwitzer.
7. Conv. R. M. Barth.
8. Conv. H. Gollwitzer.
9. Conv. R. M. Barth.
10. Conv. H. Gollwitzer.
11. Information from Dr. Lili Simon, from Corr. E. Busch, August 3, 1985.
12. Corr. M. Barth.
13. Ibid.
14. Conv. E. Busch.
15. Statement of Dr. Lili Simon, from Corr. E. Busch, August 3, 1985.
16. Conv. M. Barth.
17. Ibid.

Chapter 8: Confessing the Faith in the Church's Struggle

1. Information from Dr. Lili Simon, from Corr. E. Bush, August 3, 1985.
2. Eberhard Busch, *Karl Barth,* p. 216.
3. Conv. H. Gollwitzer.
4. Conv. E. Busch.
5. Conv. H. Gollwitzer.
6. Ibid.
7. See Hans Prolingheuer, *Der Fall Karl Barth, Chronographie einer Vertreibung 1934–1935,* p. 40, note 13.
8. See Christoph Barth, *Bekenntnis im Werden,* p. 14, note 13.
9. Ibid., p. 37.
10. A note in her journal and a letter from Barth to Thurneysen, January 8, 1934, in which he mentioned a log of this synod made by Charlotte von Kirschbaum, clearly indicate her presence. (Corr. H. Stoevesandt.)
11. Christoph Barth, op. cit., p 24, note 76.
12. Ibid., pp. 11, 20.
13. Busch, *Barth,* p. 255. In describing this gathering, Busch relied on a letter from Charlotte von Kirschbaum to Thurneysen, January 26, 1934, (see p. 168, n. 5), from which he concluded that she had been present in person.
14. Busch, *Barth,* p. 279. Here Busch makes use of a letter from Charlotte von Kirschbaum to A. Lempp, October 10, 1935 (p. 19, n.6), which indicates that she was present. See also Hans Prolingheuer, *Der Fall Karl Barth,* pp. 207, 230.
15. In *Der Fall Karl Barth,* Prolingheuer has documented Barth's banishment much more fully and vividly.
16. Prolingheuer, *Der Fall Karl Barth,* pp. 60–61.

Chapter 9: Committed Service in Swiss Exile

1. Hans Prolingheuer, *Der Fall Karl Barth,* pp. 123, 125, 166, 178, 189, 191, 199, 217, 226, 230.
2. Tel. conv. W. v. Kirschbaum, November 29, 1984.
3. Cf. H. Prolingheuer, *Kleine politische Kirchengeschichte,* p. 182, note 100.
4. Eberhard Busch, *Karl Barth,* p. 304.
5. Ibid., pp. 199 and 267, n. 4.
6. Eberhard Bethge, ed., *Dietrich Bonhoeffer—Schweitzer Korrespondenz 1941–1942,* "Im Gesprach mit Karl Barth," in the series, *Theologische Existenz heute,* no. 214, p. 15.

7. Ibid., p. 18.
8. Ibid., pp. 17, 18.
9. Ibid., pp. 17–18, 31.
10. Letters in the personal possession of Charlotte von Kirschbaum were stored in a large number of wooden and cardboard boxes and "preserved" in the attic of the Karl Barth Archives. After being undisturbed for ten years they were examined in a cursory manner in 1981, and the exchange of correspondence between Bonhoeffer and Barth/Kirschbaum came to light. There may still be other undiscovered treasures hidden there. See Bethge, op. cit., where a letter from Dr. H. Stoevesandt to Bethge is found on p. 21.
11. Tel. conv. W. v. Kirschbaum, November 29, 1984.

Chapter 10: Toward a Free and Independent Germany

1. Werner Mittenzwei, *Exil in der Schweiz,* in the series *Kunst und Literatur im antifaschistischen Exil 1933–1945,* vol. 2, p. 329.
2. See Karl Hans Bergmann, *Die Bewegung "Freies Deutschland" in der Schweiz, 1943–1945,* pp. 23–32.
3. Mittenzwei, *Exil,* p. 330.
4. Bergmann, *Die Bewegung,* p. 61.
5. Corr. W. v. Kirschbaum.
6. Bergmann, *Die Bewegung,* p. 63.
7. Mittenzwei, *Exil,* p. 336.
8. Bergmann, *Die Bewegung,* p. 156.
9. Charlotte von Kirchbaum's speech on behalf of the Movement for a Free Germany is found on pp. 81–92 of this book.
10. Eberhard Busch, *Karl Barth,* pp. 338 and 276, n. 6.
11. Ibid., pp. 338 and 273, n. 6.

Chapter 11: An Immeasurable Contribution

1. Preface to *CD* III/3, p. xiii.
2. Ibid.
3. Ibid.
4. Preface to *CD* IV/4, p. viii.
5. Karl Küpisch, *Karl Barth in Selbstzeugnissen und Bilddokumenten,* p. 104.
6. Ibid.

7. That Charlotte von Kirschbaum also did exegesis is clear from her book *Die wirkliche Frau*.
8. Conv. E. Busch.
9. Eberhard Busch, *Karl Barth*, p. 226. That Charlotte von Kirschbaum's immeasurable contribution is to be found in the fine print in the *CD* is an assumption resulting from reflections in retrospect. This assumption cannot be documented through close analysis of the text, at least not within the scope of this book. It is based on my conversations with Bush and Gollwitzer.
10. Ernst Wolf and Charlotte von Kirschbaum, eds., *Antwort. Karl Barth zum 70. Geburtstag am 10 Mai 1956*, pp. 945–960.
11. Conv. M. Barth.
12. Charlotte von Kirschbaum, *Die wirkliche Frau*, Preface.
13. See Busch, Barth, p. 377.
14. Ibid. pp. 377, 417, 458.

Chapter 12: Charlotte von Kirschbaum—"*Die wirkliche Frau*"?

1. Charlotte von Kirschbaum, *Die Wirkliche Frau*, Preface.
2. Eberhard Busch, *Karl Barth*, p. 377.
3. Any attempt to identify traces of Charlotte von Kirschbaum's writing in paragraph 45.3 of *CD* III/2 would require intensive research and language analysis, involving not only parallels but also differences. Such an undertaking lies beyond the scope of this book, and thus at this point these references must suffice.
4. Corr. M. Barth.
5. Von Kirschbaum, *Die Wirkliche Frau*, p. 34.
6. Ibid., p. 16.
7. Ibid., p. 63.
8. Ibid., p. 66.
9. Ibid., p. 83; cf. pp. 78–87.
10. Gertrud von Le Fort, *Die ewige Frau*.
11. Von Kirschbaum, *Die wirkliche Frau*, p. 68.
12. Ibid., p. 63.
13. See ibid.
14. Ibid., p. 95.
15. Ibid.
16. Ibid., p. 96.
17. A copy of the Japanese translation of *Die wirkliche Frau*

was shared with the author by Mr. Markus Wildi, librarian of the Cantonal Library in Aargau.
18. Information from Dr. Lili Simon. Corr. E. Busch, August 3, 1985.
19. C. von Kirschbaum, *Die wirkliche Frau,* Preface.

Chapter 13: As Her Strength Failed

1. See Eberhard Busch, *Karl Barth,* pp. 473–477.
2. Jürgen Fangmeier and Hinrich Stoevesandt, eds., *Karl Barth—Briefe 1961–1968,* Barth to Annie Hirzel, Locarno, November 28, 1962, p. 105.
3. Conv. M. Barth.
4. Conv. R. M. Barth.
5. Fangmeier and Stoevesandt, *Barth,* Barth to Helmut Gollwitzer, November 7, 1967, p. 446.
6. Ibid., p. 83.
7. Conv. E. Busch.
8. See Busch, *Barth,* p. 490.
9. Fangmeier and Stoevesandt, *Barth,* Barth to Helmut Gollwitzer, November 7, 1967, p. 446.
10. Ibid. Barth's circular letter to those who had congratulated him on his 82nd birthday, late May 1968, p. 748.

Chapter 14: A Long, Slow Departure

1. Corr. F. Zellweger-Barth.
2. Conv. E. Busch.
3. Conv. E. Busch.
4. Helmut Gollwitzer, "Predigt zur Beerdigung von Charlotte von Kirschbaum am 28 Juli 1975—Friedhof am Hörnli, Basel," *Nachrufe,* no. 27 in the series *Kaiser Traktate,* p. 32.
5. Ibid.
6. Ibid.
7. Conv. M. Barth.
8. Corr. F. Zellweger-Barth.
9. Gollwitzer, "Predigt," p. 34.

Bibliography

Published Works

Barth, Christoph. *Bekenntnis im Werden,* Neukirchen, 1979.
Barth, Karl. *Church Dogmatics.* ET Edinburgh: T.&T. Clark, III/2, 1960; III/3, 1960; III/4, 1961; IV/4, 1969.
Bergmann, Karl Hans. *Die Bewegung "Freies Deutschland" in der Schweiz, 1943–1945.* Munich, 1974.
Bethge, Eberhard, ed. *Dietrich Bonhoeffer—Schweizer Korrespondenz 1941–1942,* "Im Gesprach mit Karl Barth," no. 214 in the series, *Theologische Existenz heute.* Munich, 1982.
Brochure of the movement "Freies Deutschland," *Um Deutschlands nachste Zukunft.* Zurich, 1945.
Busch, Eberhard. *Karl Barth: His Life from Letters and Autobiographical Texts* (ET). Philadelphia: Fortress Press, 1976.
Casalis, Georges. *Karl Barth, Person und Werk.* Darmstadt, 1960.
Fangmeier, Jürgen, and Hinrich Stoevesandt, eds. *Karl Barth—Briefe 1961–1968.* Zurich, 1975.
Gollwitzer, Helmut. *Nachrufe,* no. 27 in the series *Kaiser Traktate.* Munich, 1977.
Illich, Ivan. *Vom Recht auf Gemeinheit.* Hamburg, 1982.
Kirschbaum, Charlotte von. *Der Dienst der Frau in der Wortverkündigung,* in *Theologische Studien* 30–40, ed. by Karl Barth. Zurich, 1951.
———. *Die wirkliche Frau.* Zurich, 1949.
Koch, Dieter, ed. *Offene Briefe 1945–1968.* Zurich, 1984.
Küppers, Erica. "Auf dem Bergli," in *Stimme der Gemeinde,* 1966, columns 299–302.
Küpish, Karl. *Karl Barth in Selbstzeugnissen und Bilddokumenten.* Stuttgart, 1977.

Le Fort, Gertrud von. *Die ewige Frau.* Munich, 1934.
Mittenzwei, Werner. *Exil in der Schweiz,* vol. 2 in the series *Kunst und Literatur im antifaschistischen Exil 1933–1945.* Frankfurt, 1981.
Popge, Michael, ed. *Schreien nach Gerechtigkeit, Gertrud Staewen zum 90 Geburtstag.* Berlin, 1984.
Prolingheuer, Hans. *Der Fall Karl Barth 1934–1935, Chronographie einer Vertreibung,* 2nd ed. Neukirchen, 1984.
———. *Kleine politische Kirchengeschichte.* Cologne, 1984.
Thurneysen, Eduard, ed. *Karl Barth–Eduard Thurneysen, Briefwechsel 1921–1930.* Zurich, 1974.
Wehr, Gerhard. *Karl Barth: Theologe und Gottes fröhlicher Partisan.* Gütersloh, 1979.
Wolf, Ernst, and Charlotte von Kirschbaum, eds. *Antwort. Karl Barth zum 70. Geburtstag am 10 Mai, 1956.* Zollikon-Zurich, 1956.

Unpublished Sources

1. Personal Conversations

Conv. M. Barth: Dr. Markus Barth, son of Karl Barth and professor of New Testament Theology, Basel, July 26, 1984.
Conv. R. M. Barth: Rose Marie Barth, daughter-in-law of Karl Barth and friend of Charlotte von Kirschbaum, July 26, 1984.
Conv. E. Busch: Dr. Eberhard Busch, Pastor in Uerkheim, Switzerland, former assistant to Karl Barth and author of the major biography of Karl Barth, July 31, 1984.
Conv. H. Gollwitzer: Dr. Helmut Gollwitzer, Professor of Protestant Theology at the Free University of Berlin and lecturer in Systematic Theology at the Church College, Berlin, November 8, 1984.
Conv. W. v. Kirschbaum: Wolf von Kirschbaum, nephew of Charlotte von Kirschbaum, Kiefersfelden, September 13, 1984.
Tel. conv. W. v. Kirschbaum: Telephone conversations with Wolf von Kirschbaum, November 29, 1984, and March 15, 1985.

2. Personal Correspondence

Corr. M. Barth: Letter from Prof. Markus Barth to the author, March 21, 1985.

Unpublished Sources 153

Corr. E. Busch: Letters from Dr. Eberhard Busch to the author, July 17 and August 3, 1985.
Corr. G. Casalis: Letter from Professor Georges Casalis to the author, December 14, 1985.
Corr. W. v. Kirschbaum: Letter from Wolf von Kirschbaum, nephew of Charlotte von Kirschbaum, to the author, December 16, 1984.
Corr. H. Stoevesandt: Letter from Dr. Hinrich Stoevesandt, director of the Karl Barth Archives, Basel, to the author, January 24, 1985.
Corr. F. Zellweger-Barth: Letter from Mrs. Franziska Zellweger-Barth, daughter of Karl Barth, to the author, May 10, 1985.

3. Unpublished Documents

Unpub. doc. Barth family: Memorial reminiscences of Charlotte von Kirschbaum, written by Karl Barth's children.
Unpub. doc. W. v. Kirschbaum: Obituary of Maximilian von Kirschbaum, father of Charlotte von Kirschbaum, in the possession of Wolf von Kirschbaum.
Unpub doc. G. Staewen: Reminiscences of Gertrud Staewen, former staff member of the Church Institute for Social Justice, Tegel, Berlin, concerning her friend Charlotte von Kirschbaum, in the possession of Dr. Helmet Gollwitzer, Berlin.

Index of Names

Abegg, Wilhelm, 55
Asmussen, Hans, 48

Barth, Christoph, 47, 70, 135
Barth, Franziska, *see* Zellweger-Barth
Barth, Fritz, 112
Barth, Markus, 12, 16, 70, 135
Barth, Nelly, 31, 39–40, 74–75, 132–133, 138
Barth, Robert Matthias, 26
Barth, Rose Marie, 12, 15–17 (quoted), 42, 128
Beauvoir, Simone de, 37, 60, 62, 67
Beck, Ludwig, 53
Bleibtreu, Otto, 50
Bonhoeffer, Dietrich, 51, 53
Bousset, Wilhelm, 108
Breit, Thomas, 48
Buck, Pearl S., 112
Busch, Eberhard, 12, 64, 71, 130, 132

Calvin, Jean, 103, 111, 129
Casalis, Georges, 135, 140
Churchill, Winston, 84

Delling, Gerhard, 112

Eichholz, Georg, 46

Fliedner, Friederike, 131
Frick, Hans, 125
Fürst, Walther, 46

Giesen, Elisabeth, 132
Giesen, Martin, 132
Gisevius, Hans Bernd, 53
Gogarten, Friedrich, 26
Gollwitzer, Brigitte, 33
Gollwitzer, Helmut, 12, 46, 71, 73, 75, 130, 133

Handrich, Karl, 133
Heinemann, Gustav, 75
Herrmann, Gertrud, 103
Hitler, Adolf, 48–49, 67, 81–82, 84–85, 87–88
Howard, R. W., 123

Immer, Karl, 48

Jacobs, Helene, 33
Jaspers, Karl, 137

Kant, Immanuel, 42
Kierkegaard, Sören, 35
Kirschbaum, Hans von, 23
Kirschbaum, Henriette von, 23
Kirschbaum, Max von, 23
Kirschbaum, Maximilian von, 23
Kirschbaum, Wolf von, 12
Kloppenburg, Heinz, 46

Koch, Werner, 46, 131
Kreck, Walter, 46
Krushchev, Nikita, 137
Küppers, Erica, 46, 49
Kupisch, Karl, 59

Langhoff, Wolfgang, 54–55
Lanzenstiel, Georg, 46
Leenhardt, Franz Josef, 119, 121
Le Fort, Gertrud von, 62, 66–67
Lempp, Albert, 29
Lentrodt, Emmy, 23
Lietzmann, Hans, 108
Lilje, Hans, 127–128
Luther, Martin, 35, 109, 129

Mann, Thomas, 25
Marahrens, August, 49, 125, 127–128
Marquardt, Friedrich-Wilhelm, 33
Merz, Georg, 25–29, 32, 39, 47, 134
Merz, Johannes, 134

Niemöller, Martin, 15, 49
Niesel, Wilhelm, 103

Oster, Hans, 53

Pestalozzi, Gerty, 28, 36
Pestalozzi, Rudolf (Ruedi), 28, 30, 36
Prolingheuer, Hans, 11–13
Przywara, Erich, 35

Ratzinger, Josef, 137
Rust, Bernhard, 50
Rodenhausen, Petra, 14
Röhr, Esther, 13
Rolfhaus, Wilhelm, 103

Salomon, Otto, 55
Sasse, Hermann, 48
Schlatter, Adolf, 106
Schlier, Heinrich, 105
Scholz, Heinrich, 41–42
Schütt, Leni, 127
Schulte, Hannelies, 94
Schwarz, Martin, 73
Schweizer, Eduard, 95, 99–100, 119, 122
Simon, Lili, 12, 46
Staewen, Gertrud, 33, 36
Stalin, Josef, 84, 137
Steck, Karl Gerhard, 46
Steinmetz, Melanie, 33
Sticker, Anna, 131
Stoll, Klaus-Dieter, 130

Thurneysen-Casalis, Dorothee, 135, 136, 138
Thurneysen, Eduard, 16, 26, 28, 29, 31–33, 35, 41, 44, 132, 135
Thurneysen, Marguerite, 132
Traub, Hellmut, 46
Trotsky, Leo, 137

Vilmar, August Friedrich Christian, 101–102
Vogel, Heinrich, 137
Voltaire, 137

Wehr, Gerhard, 22
Wildi, Markus, 134–135
Winzen, Peter, 13
Wolf, Ernst, 60, 133
Wolf, Uvo, 133

Zellweger-Barth, Franziska (Fränzeli), 41, 135
Zellweger-Barth, Max, 73

www.ingramcontent.com/pod-product-compliance
Lightning Source LLC
Chambersburg PA
CBHW072144160426
43197CB00012B/2235